THE CONTEMPORARY
flower
arranger

THE CONTEMPORARY
flower arranger

A fresh, new approach to creating glorious displays

LYNDA OWEN

CHARTWELL
BOOKS, INC.

A QUINTET BOOK

Published by Chartwell Books

A Division of Book Sales, Inc.

114 Northfield Avenue

Edison, New Jersey 08837

ISBN 0-7858-1020-X

This book was designed and produced by

Quintet Publishing Limited

6 Blundell Street

London N7 9BH

Creative Director: **Richard Dewing**

Art Director: **Silke Braun**

Designer: **Jacqui Ellis-Dodds**

Project Editor: **Kate Yeates**

Editor: **Deborah Gray**

Photographer: **Philip Wilkins**

Typeset in Great Britain by

Central Southern Typesetters, Eastbourne

Manufactured in China by Regent Publishing Services Ltd

Printed in China by Leefung-Asco Printers Trading Limited

Contents

introduction

Imagine a world with no flowers. Never to see a tree in blossom, a drift of nodding daffodils, or the elegance of a single stem of Madonna lilies. Floral magic surrounds us; it's a wild flower meadow, a regiment of bedding plants in a city park, it's the unexpected first blossom that heralds spring's arrival. So it comes as no surprise that throughout history artists have used flowers as their inspiration, and however poor, everyone has taken pleasure in cutting a few precious blooms and creating a little piece of nature in a vase. No matter that it is not a lasting keepsake, but a fleeting pleasure, and once gone can never be recreated exactly: the transient identity of each design is part of a flower arrangement's intrinsic beauty.

In the hustle and bustle of modern day life a bowl of flowers in our homes or work place has never been more important. Tremendous emphasis is now placed on color and furnishings, and floral art can be the cheapest form of interior design. The environment we live in dictates our approach to creativity. Even the most soulless space can be given a lift with a few well-placed blooms. One or two leafy branches will produce an oasis of calm in

a busy modern office; strewing rose petals across a candlelit dinner-table gives an ethereal moody atmosphere, just right for a romantic tryst; a minimalist approach with a few bold exotic flowers will give a chic, contemporary, beauty to a modern apartment. Whatever the mood, whether it is soothing or dynamic, calming or vibrant, any feeling or emotion can be portrayed with flowers. You can transform a room into a wonderland at very little expense.

The quality of flowers has improved enormously in the thirty years I have been a florist. When I first started out there was one variety of red rose available and two varieties of pink to choose from, with stems so weak they could hardly hold the head up. Now there are hundreds of tints and tones of every imaginable color in any variety of flower you can think of.

Given my years as a florist you might be forgiven for thinking I would be a little jaded and have seen it all, but it is still a pleasure to work with nature's most wonderful gifts. When I open that first box of narcissi that means winter is almost over, or the heavenly scent of sweet peas fills the shop first thing in the morning, or one perfectly formed rose catches the eye, it makes me realize how lucky I am to be a florist.

In the past, flower arrangements were stereotyped and unimaginative, but in recent years there has been a revival of creativity, and new concepts of style and technique are emerging. More emphasis is placed on the shape and texture of flowers, their color and the way they grow naturally. Flowers are arranged freely and inspiration is taken from nature to produce exciting new styles.

It is important to view each flower with a fresh attitude, taking in the beauty of the stem, the texture of the leaf, the color and shape of the flower head, all these elements will ultimately determine how the flower is best arranged. Sometimes one perfect flower on its

own in a vase will have more impact and make more of a statement than a huge bunch of blooms. Changing our attitude, seeing flowers with different eyes, is the first step to a more creative approach to flower arranging.

Excellent craftsmanship is also important. New concepts and techniques mean learning new skills and developing different methods to hold the flowers in place. Technical skills will help build confidence in your own ability. The knowledge that your floral creation is well made will help you become more creative, choosing flowers will be a pleasurable experience instead of a minefield of indecisions and ultimately you will produce better all-round designs to delight your family and friends.

Inspiration can come from many sources. It creeps up on us at the least expected times, or appears in a flash of brilliance. When

we want it most it often fails us, so it is worthwhile storing up good ideas to use at later dates. Sketch the ideas if necessary.

Inspiration is all around, in nature, the flowers themselves, past and contemporary fashions and styles; its up to us to nurture it. Some people are born with an inbuilt sense of style and creativity, for others skills need to be forged gradually. Start with simple designs which will build confidence and develop practical knowledge, enabling you to successfully tackle more demanding projects later. In this book the arrangements have been devised at differing skill levels, you can gradually build up from the easy designs to intermediate before moving on to more demanding arrangements that require greater depth of knowledge.

Above all is the enjoyment you get from creating your truly original design. Having fun with flowers is the priority and you will find the more relaxed you are, the more original and artistic your arrangements will become.

Let us now explore together the glorious creative world of flower arrangement.

one

MATERIALS & TECHNIQUES

YOUR DESIGNS CAN BE WONDERFUL, INSPIRED CREATIONS OF YOUR IMAGINATION, STATE-OF-THE-ART LIVING SCULPTURES, BUT IF THE FOUNDATIONS OF THE ARRANGEMENT ARE NOT FIRM, IF THE FLOWERS FALL OUT OF THE FOAM, IF THERE IS NOT ENOUGH WATER IN THE CONTAINER, OR THE CORRECT BALANCE HAS NOT BEEN ACHIEVED, THEN YOUR DESIGN IS WORTHLESS. YOUR FIRST IMPORTANT STEPS IN FLOWER ARRANGEMENT ARE LEARNING THE BASIC TECHNIQUES AND PRACTICING GOOD WORKMANSHIP. THIS CHAPTER IS THE MOST IMPORTANT OF ALL. HOW TO CHOOSE YOUR FLOWERS, SKILLFULLY BLEND COLORS, MASTER THE FUNDAMENTAL ASSEMBLY TECHNIQUES AND BASIC PRINCIPLES OF GOOD DESIGN, ALL REQUIRE CONSTANT PRACTICE. ONCE LEARNT THOROUGHLY HOWEVER, THESE ELEMENTS OF GOOD WORKMANSHIP WILL ALWAYS BE A SOUND BASIS TO WORK FROM.

choosing flowers

Choosing the flowers is the first step to creating a wonderful arrangement. It is the most important decision you will make and should not be done in haste. Think about what type of arrangement you are going to make; the container you will use, the color scheme and the quantity of flowers needed before you go to purchase the flowers.

Here, flowers are massed ready to be auctioned. From the moment they are picked flowers are cared for and conditioned to ensure their quality and longevity.

With increased technology in flower production the vase life of flowers has improved greatly. Many flowers now have pre-treatment with flower foods, when they are cut by growers, to increase their life span. Most flowers are transported in water in specially cooled vehicles, again to ensure the flowers last longer and retain their quality.

You will want your flowers to last as long as possible so always buy the best quality flowers you possibly can, and from a reputable source. Flowers displayed outside might look pretty but the flowers have to battle against the elements to survive. A cool shop or temperature controlled surroundings where the flowers are cared for, is the best place to purchase.

Your local florist is the best person to go to for advice. As a professional, she is well qualified to assist you and help you make the right choice, and recommend the best buy. Develop a relationship with your florist who will also want your flowers to last as long as possible, so that you will return again and again.

Flowers are best bought from a shop where they are looked after properly. It is well worth cultivating a relationship with your local florist who will be able to give you advice, particularly on the best buys.

Once you start buying flowers regularly you will soon recognize good quality. Sometimes it can be as bad to buy an immature flower as a fully open one. Flowers should not be bought in tight bud. If the flower is too immature it will never develop fully. Lilies, roses, iris, tulips, freesia, and alstroemeria in particular will never reach their full potential if they are cut from the plant before the buds have fully developed.

Most of all, enjoy the experience of browsing and purchasing in a florist's shop which holds irresistible displays of super flowers.

caring for flowers

Cutting a flower stem

1 Hold the knife firmly in one hand, and the flower near the base of the stem in the other. Make a long diagonal cut. To prevent accidents, always cut away from yourself.

2 Once the stem has been cut it should be put immediately into water.

How you care for the flowers once you get them home will also determine their length of life. Try not to leave flowers out of water for too long. Once home, the stems will need recutting and the flowers will need to be given a long drink before they are arranged.

Foliage is often something that is forgotten and a few leaves are hastily picked from the garden at the last minute. Without foliage a flower arrangement looks stark, bare, and unnatural. You must learn to value it as an integral part of any design. There is a wealth of greenery to choose from, both commercially grown or picked from the garden. Cut garden foliage in the morning if possible and never in the heat of the day. Foliage needs careful conditioning if it is to remain vivid and long lasting. Most foliage benefits from being submerged in water for a short period, or placed in buckets of deep water to revive before arranging. Gray foliage however should not be submerged as it will lose its grayness when under water.

Always use a knife to cut flower and foliage stems where possible. A short-handled knife with a blade approximately 2½ inches in length is perfect. A knife will give a cleaner cut than scissors, which crush and bruise the stem ends. Make a diagonal cut to expose as much of the cell structure inside the stem as possible. This enables a free flow of water and nutrients up the stem, and makes it easier to insert the stem into foam. Always take great care when using a knife, and cut away from you. Never leave a knife lying around where children or pets may find it.

Flower food will help to keep the flowers at their peak for longer. It is available from florists and is a combination of sugars and chemicals which is added to the water to aid longevity. Use as directed by the manufacturer's instructions on the packet. Finally, bacteria kills flowers faster than anything else, so keeping the container clean and changing the water regularly will also help the flowers have a longer life.

choosing a container

Glass vases and bottles are great containers for flower arranging, especially for the beginner. Bottles can be grouped or used individually, with just a few flowers used to make a simple but striking arrangement.

Modern pots come in all shapes, sizes and colors and can add an exciting dimension to your arrangement. Remember to think through the color scheme and make sure the flowers and container harmonize.

Often, it is not until a bunch of flowers arrives in our hands that the search starts for a receptacle to put them in. Sometimes flowers are put into the nearest container without further thought, and the result seems for some reason not quite right. If we were baking a cake and put it into the wrong size tin the result would be disaster, and the same applies to flowers and their holder.

The container is an integral part of any flower arrangement and should complement the flowers perfectly. So before purchasing the flowers, think about the vases you have at home and buy flowers which will look good in one of them.

When choosing vases think about the room they will be displayed in and choose a style which will suit the decor. When starting out, buy plain vases in simple shapes and a variety of sizes as these will be the most versatile. Neutral colored containers will prove to be classic all-rounders: earth colors, greens, creams and browns will team with any flower naturally. Clear glass vases are also a good basic buy.

As the projects in this book clearly demonstrate, a vase is not the only style of container fit for flowers. Bottles, baskets, old wooden crates, terracotta urns, bowls, jugs and buckets can all work with the right combination of flowers and foliage. In fact almost any watertight container can be used. Battered old vases or plain plastic bowls can be dressed up with fabric and even wrapped in leaves to make them into perfectly presentable containers. Experiment and see what great ideas you can come up with.

When choosing flowers and foliage for your container, look at the size of it, and buy flowers of a suitable size and shape. As a general rule, the best length for the flowers is twice the height of the container. Again, with practice, you will learn to judge the right length of stem for the container you are using and the design being created.

elements of design

In floral art, you do not want to be too restricted by rules and regulations on how to arrange flowers. Developing your own style and using the eye to measure what looks good is the best discipline of all. The principles of design, scale, proportion, balance, harmony and rhythm are there as guidelines, they form a framework of support for the artist, they are not to be rigidly obeyed.

This does not mean however that you start with no plan of how the arrangement will look when finished. On the contrary, you should always have a clear idea in your head of the finished design, and in this way you will not deviate and add flowers unnecessarily. To start with, simplicity is the key to success.

A modern approach can be given to the most traditionally styled arrangements, to achieve an open natural look, rather than the stiff symmetrical shapes of yesteryear. Start by thinking about the outline. Look at the materials you have to use, and think how you will make the best of them, showing them off to the greatest advantage. As a general guideline, make the flowers twice the height of the container. As you become more experienced your eye will tell you what looks the best. Remember, this is art, rigid measurements do not apply.

Choose the flowers and foliage for the look you wish to achieve. To create an open country style arrangement for example, use lots of foliage; garden materials make a lush background for country style flowers. In a modern design the form of the flowers is very important, so choose flowers with strong architectural shapes and bold leaves to create such an arrangement.

Recessing some flowers low into the center and sides of the arrangement will give the design more depth. Using flowers at different heights within the design will also heighten the interest. Learn to group flowers for greater impact. By making groups within the design of one type of flower you will maximize their visual impact.

When all the elements are in harmony, the results can be breath-taking.

Always have a clear idea in your head of the design before you start arranging the material.

color

Of all the elements of design color has the most immediate impact. Nothing can catch the imagination, inspire a theme, or create a mood quite like color. It can make subtle suggestions or outrageous statements: it can be cool and tranquil, or hot and fiery; it can imply differing meanings and suggest the various seasons of the year.

Clever use of color is something that can be learned. Studying nature is one of the best ways of exploring color as it is in nature that the most wonderful color schemes can be found. Think of the sunrise and brilliant sunsets or a rainbow after a storm. Look at a bird's feather and examine the minute and intricate tints and tones of color, or the infinite combinations of green in a variegated leaf. A basic understanding of color theory will help you create effective color schemes.

Combining colors into recognized color harmonies can be achieved with the color wheel. The color wheel shows how colors relate to each other and which work well together. It is worthwhile studying it to increase your awareness of color and help you choose interesting color schemes.

It is most important that you enjoy color. Trial and experiment are essential, and too much strict observance of the rules can inhibit your natural flair. Fashions in color change with the season, which should encourage you to try something new. Remember creative color harmonies are an art form in themselves, so be creative.

The primary colors of red, yellow, and blue are pure colors and cannot be produced from other colors. From these three colors all others are mixed (with the exception of black and white). These pure colors are strong and vibrant.

The secondary colors are orange, green, and violet. They are mixed from equal proportions of two primary colors.

Complementary color scheme
Colors that contrast with one another are positioned exactly opposite one another on the color wheel and are called complementary colors, for example, yellow and purple. If colors are used at their full strength it can be exciting and vibrant, as the colors intensify each other.

The color wheel shows how colors relate to each other and is therefore a useful guide when choosing a color scheme.

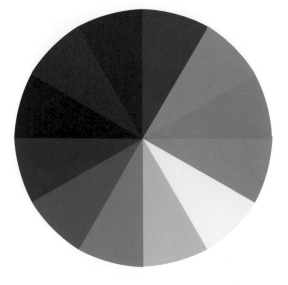

texture

Texture in floral art is used to add interest to an arrangement. If all the flowers and foliage are one texture, then the look will be bland and uninteresting. Using different textures within a design will heighten its visual appeal. Flowers come in an enormous range of textures, from smooth lilies to busy cow parsley, delicately crumpled poppies to velvety anemones. Even when using just one variety of flower, additional texture can be introduced through foliage. Shiny foliage will attract the eye more than other textures, so is best placed at focal areas.

Using a variety of textures will add interest to the design.

form

The use of different shaped flowers and foliages will also add interest to an arrangement. Flowers are divided into three basic shapes: round or focal flowers such as roses, carnations, and gerberas; line materials such as delphiniums, gladioli, equisetum, and transitional shapes such as spray chrysanthemums, lizianthus, and cornflowers which act as stepping stones, linking the other two shapes together within the arrangement. A balanced design will use flowers from at least two, if not all three, of these groups.

Vertical and horizontal lines combine with round and flat shapes, to create a study in form.

space

Space defines and accentuates the shapes of flowers used. There is a fine balance between leaving too much space in an arrangement and cramming the flowers and foliage together producing a cluttered, undefined shape. Learning to use space effectively in a design takes time and practice but makes all the different to the end result. After a while your eye will automatically spot a gap which is just right for an extra flower, or an area of your design which needs a little less foliage. Space is valuable in an arrangement, and as you go along you will learn to appreciate its design qualities.

Like a bird in flight the calla lilies soar above the container in a study of visual balance.

essential equipment

There are certain tools and equipment which are essential in floral art, and it is much easier if they are all kept together in a small workbox. Without these tools and equipment it would be difficult to perform all the tasks required, so always keep them to hand when doing an arrangement. It is also advisable to keep tools clean and in good working order.

Cutting and gluing tools

The main tools you need are for cutting and it is important to have the right blade for the job. Make sure you take adequate safety precautions when using a knife or scissors and don't leave them lying around after use. A glue gun is fast becoming essential equipment for floral art. It can glue dried materials and accessories in minutes. The glue emitted is very hot and can burn the skin, so extreme care must be taken when using the glue gun.

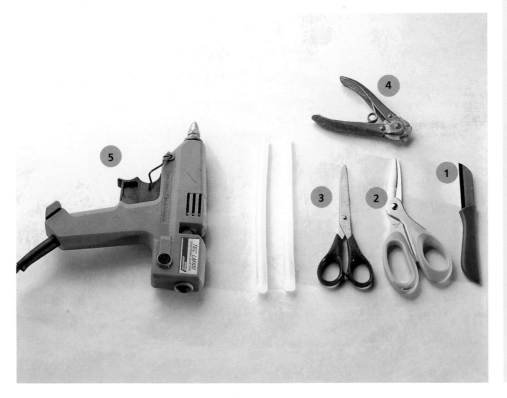

1 Florist's knife
A knife is the most important tool as it is used for most cutting jobs. Professional florists use a knife to cut stems as it gives a cleaner cut than scissors and is quicker to use. You can hold a knife in the hand while performing other tasks, with scissors you have to keep putting them down. Choose a knife with a short blade and a handle that is shaped to the hand slightly. Take care when using cutting implements and put away when not in use.

2 Florist's scissors
There are many good designs on the market. Always buy the best quality as these will last much longer than cheaper versions. Choose a sturdy pair of scissors with handles which feel comfortable and easy to hold. Clippers can also be useful to have to hand for cutting thick, woody stems.

3 Ribbon scissors
 It is not advisable to cut ribbon or fabric with floristry scissors as these will tear the material. A small pair of ribbon scissors will give a more precise cut.

4 Wire cutters
 If floristry scissors are used to cut wires they will soon become blunt and unusable. Wire cutters will cut any thickness of wire and are invaluable to the flower arranger.

5 Glue gun
This electrical appliance heats solid glue to liquid form and emits small quantities of the liquid glue when a trigger is pressed. The glue dries quickly, and only a small amount is necessary to stick items together.

floral foam

This is indispensable to the flower arranger, it is used as the support for the majority of arrangements. It comes in two forms, one for use with dried and artificial flowers, the other is used wet with cut flowers. Both types of foam are easily cut to fit with a knife. Never skimp with foam, as it will break if too many stems are pushed into a small area, and always discard after use.

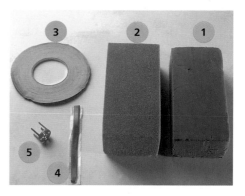

1 Wet floral foam
For use with cut flowers which must have water to survive. The foam is full of air pockets which fill with water once submerged.

2 Dry floral foam
This is for use with dried and artificial flowers and like the wet foam can be cut to shape.

3 Florist's adhesive tape
This is mainly used to fix the foam into the container. The tape fastens to either side of the container, keeping the foam in place. The sides of the container must be completely dry for the tape to stick.

4 Florist's fixing tape
This is a sticky strip of adhesive which will anchor items together firmly.

5 Foam holders
Small green foam holders which florist's call "frogs," have four prongs which will anchor the foam to the base. A small piece of florist's fixing adhesive is placed on the bottom of the holder to keep the holder firmly attached to the container. The foam is then pushed onto the four prongs.

soaking foam

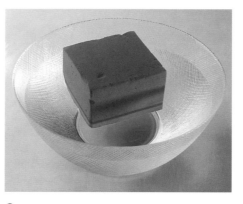

1 Cut the foam to the size required to fit the container. Fill a deep bowl with water.

2 Place the foam on top of the water. As the water is taken into the foam it will sink into the water. Never force the foam under the water.

3 Once the top of the foam is level with the water the foam is ready to use. This takes only a few seconds.

tying and fixing materials

Tying strings are part of the essential equipment for a flower arranger. Green twine, string, and raffia (1, 2, 3) are all necessary when making hand tied bouquets and for tying flowers and foliage together. Adhesive tape and double-sided tape (4, 5) are useful for sticking leaves to containers and for anchorage in glass, where it is unobtrusive.

wires and tapes

Wires play an important role in floral art. Wires enable us to manipulate and bend stems and flower heads, help support stems which might be bent or weak, and are used to provide firm anchorage into bases and containers.

Wires are chosen for their thickness and length, and choosing the right gauge of wire is important. Too strong a wire will make the flower seem rigid and unnatural, too light a wire and it will not give the support required. Wires can be purchased with a green plastic coating or a silver covering already on them, and these are ideal for support wiring flowers. Reel wires also come in a variety of gauges, some are decorative and colored. The most commonly used wires are shown in the chart below.

An assortment of wires, gutter percha tape, and ready-made hairpins.

taping a wire

Wires without a green coating often need to be covered. Wires can rust easily and a protective coating is necessary to ensure damage does not occur. A bare wire can also look unsightly. Gutter percha is a florist's tape which is used to cover wires. It is water resistant and will stretch slightly when pulled. Wires can be taped together in the same way.

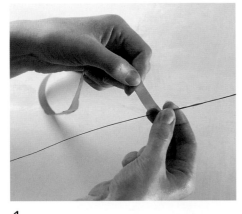

1 Start to cover the wire by wrapping the tape around the top of the wire, stretching it slightly and using your thumb and first finger to twist it round the wire. The gutter percha self seals on the wire.

2 Work down the wire, stretching the tape with one hand while twisting the tape down the wire with the thumb and first finger of the other hand. To finish off at the end of the wire, give an extra twist and cut the tape.

WIRE GAUGE CHART

gauge	imperial	metric
	18 swg	1.25 mm
	20 swg	0.90 mm
	22 swg	0.71 mm
	24 swg	0.56 mm
	26 swg	0.46 mm
	28 swg	0.38 mm
	30 swg	0.32 mm
Lengths	7 inches	180 mm
	10 inches	260 mm
	12 inches	310 mm
	14 inches	360 mm
	18 inches	460 mm

hairpins

Hairpins are useful for pinning moss and leaves onto foam. They are easily made by cutting a wire into equal length pieces, and then bending to form a hairpin. The length and gauge of wire used depends on the size, weight and density of material to be pinned, but generally 22 swg, 12 inch wires are used. Alternatively hairpins can be bought. They are sometimes called German pins and have sharp pointed ends which are ideal for pinning.

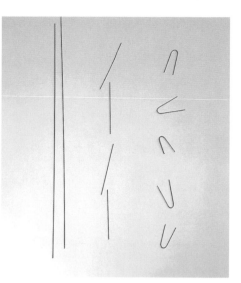

To make hairpins simply cut a wire into equal lengths and fold the lengths in half.

support wiring

When a stem is too weak to hold the flower head, or bends in an unsuitable direction, a discreet support wire can help to control the flower, making it easier to use.

The lightest wire possible should be used. Generally for most stems 22 swg and 24 swg are the most efficient, but this will depend on the weight of the flower and stem. A heavier or lighter gauge might have to be used.

1 Use a 22 swg wire, 18 inches in length.

2 Insert the wire into the stem approximately 2 inches from the head. Push the wire gently but firmly up the inside of the stem and into the seed box.

3 Twist the remaining external wire around the stem neatly. The head of the flower can now be gently manipulated, until the stem is straight, or the flower head is tilted in the direction required.

stitching a leaf

To support wire leaves a stitch method is used.

1 Use a silver or green coated wire 30 swg, 7 inches in length. Make a small stitch three quarters of the way up the main vein.

2 Pull the wire through until equal amounts show either side of the stitch. Bring both wires down to the base of the leaf.

3 Wind one wire around the other wire and the top of the stem twice, leaving two legs of wire.

double-leg mount wire

A double-leg mount wire is used extensively as a form of wiring in floristry. It has many uses, the most important of which is anchoring foliage into a base or floral foam.

3 Wrap one leg firmly around the stem and other leg twice.

1 Take a small group of cupressus, approximately 2½ inches in length, and a 7 inch 20 swg wire.

2 Bend the wire in half and place at the back of the cupressus.

4 Once wired there should be two wire legs.

wiring a rose button-hole

A rose button-hole can be worn at any time by both women and men. It is a nice gift at a dinner party, placed on the plate just before guests arrive at the dinner table, using a color to complement the decor.

1 Choose a perfectly shaped rose with no blemishes. Cut the stem leaving approximately ½ inch at the top. Using a 7 inch 22 swg wire, push the wire into the top of the stem and on into the seed box of the rose, then wrap the wire around the top of the stem once.

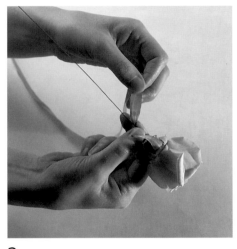

2 Then gutter tape from the top of the stem down the wire (see page 18). Wire three rose leaves using the stitching method (see page 20), then gutter tape the stems.

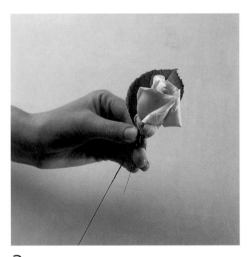

3 Take a rose leaf and place it at the back of the flower, holding the stem just below the rose head.

4 Place two more leaves to the sides of the rose. Use a silver wire to secure the leaves and rose together at the top of the stem.

5 Cut the wire stem to approximately 2½ inches in length. Then gutter tape down the stem from top to bottom concealing all wires and making sure no wires protrude from the end of the stem.

6 Face the rose by tilting the head forward slightly, spray with water, then add a pin.

bow making

Often, ribbon can be added to an arrangement to enhance the design. The ribbon should be an integral part of the design, and not just an item that fills a space when flowers have run out. Making a figure-of-eight bow is easy to master with a little practice. The size of the bow will depend on the proportions of the arrangement.

1 Make a loop, leaving a trail of ribbon, and hold between the thumb and fingers.

3 Pinch the ribbon together in the center of the bow.

5 Pinch the wire ends together with the loops pulled forward into the hand. Twist the wires firmly together at the back of the bow.

2 Bring the ribbon over to form another loop, holding both loops in the center. Make two more loops in this figure-of-eight style.

4 Take a 10 inch 24 swg green coated wire. Place the center of the wire onto the center of the ribbon and bend back the wire.

6 Pull out the loops to form a bow, with two wire legs for securing into moss or foam.

bouquet bows

When making hand-tied bouquets, a bow is needed with ribbon ties to wrap

around the tying point to conceal it and to be decorative.

3 Pull the loops forward into the hand, then bring the tying ribbon to the back of the bow, and tie in a firm knot.

1 Make a bow in a figure-of-eight method (as shown on page 22). Take a long length of the same ribbon, enough to tie around the tying point of the hand-tied bouquet.

2 Place the bow in the center of the ribbon tie, folding the tie in half lengthwise if the ribbon is too wide to fit comfortably.

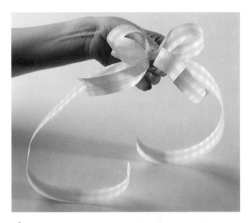

4 Pull out the ribbon loops to make a decorative shape, the long ties are now ready to wrap around the hand-tied bouquet.

making a hand-tied bouquet

Hand-tied designs need a little practice to perfect, but once the basic principles

have been mastered, many different styles of bouquet can be made.

1 Clean all the stems and remove any foliage which will be below the tying point. Lay out the flowers in groups on a table, this will enable easy access when making the bouquet.

2 Start with a small group of bushy foliage. If you are right handed, hold in the left hand and feed stems into the bouquet with the right hand. If left handed, do the reverse.

3 Build up the bouquet by adding the central flowers, in this case, centaurea. Then add eringium to fill out the bouquet and support the central flowers. The height of the flowers above the hand will depend on the size and quantity of the flowers. For this bouquet the height is approximately eight inches. The stems will start to spiral if placed from left to right at the front and from right to left at the back of the bouquet.

4 Keep adding greenery to fill out the bouquet, then start to add the smaller flowers, here cornflowers and hypericum, placing them between the central flowers in pleasing patterns.

5 Gradually bring the flowers down at the sides toward the tying point to give a good rounded profile, keeping the stems spiralling. Finish with a collar of foliage which will neaten the underside of the bouquet and give support to the flowers.

6 Once the bouquet is finished, take a long length of tying twine, double it and pass it around the stems, thread the two ends through the loop.

7 To tie the bouquet, rest it on the edge of a table. Divide the ends of the twine and pull them tightly in opposite directions. Wrap the twine firmly around the tying point, again pulling tightly, then tie in a double knot. It is important that the tie point is firm, otherwise the bouquet will disintegrate once stood up.

8 Keep the bouquet in the same position on the edge of the table. Take a bow made in the method on page 23. Place the bow at the front of the bouquet, pass the ribbon ties around the tie point, bringing them together above the bow, pull firmly and tie securely in a double knot. Rearrange the bow neatly.

9 The stems are an important part of the bouquet, either cut to fit into the chosen vase, or leave the stem length approximately one third the size of the finished bouquet. Cut the stems into an inverted "V" shape and the bouquet will stand on its own.

twig ball

Twig balls can be purchased from florist shops ready-made in a variety of sizes. However they are easy to assemble when you want a particular size or density. They can be made with a variety of vines and twigs. Choose pliable stems which will bend easily without snapping. Here, clematis vine and willow twigs are used. Soaking vines in water will aid manipulation. Even a small ball needs quite a lot of twigs and vines to produce a well-rounded sphere.

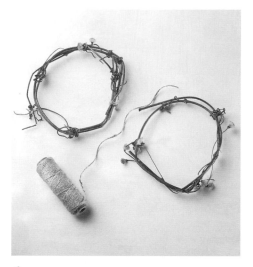

1 Make two circles of vine to the size the finished ball should be. Entwine the vine and tie firmly with string.

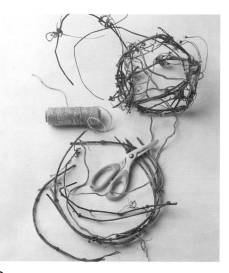

3 Start threading and weaving other vines and twigs through the ball outline to form interesting patterns.

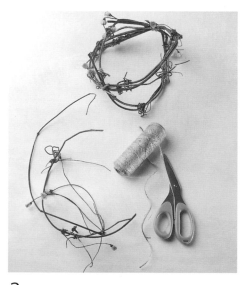

2 Push the one circle through the other to make a ball shape. Tie neatly together.

4 There should be no need to use any more string as the vines will support each other. If the twigs are too dense it is difficult to thread stems through it.

In this book the projects are designed to stimulate your interest, and help you achieve a creative flow of ideas. The quantities and varieties of flowers used are a guideline only, they need not be strictly adhered to. There is no need to rigidly copy the arrangements, hopefully they will motivate and inspire you to experiment as you progress, then you will create your own unique designs.

Use the flowers naturally, look at the way they grow and try to emulate this because nature shows us the way to make the finest design statements. It is easy to put a few flowers together and make them look wonderful, so don't feel inhibited by the flowers. Remember this is art, it has no boundaries, no limitations. It is the thrill of creating something of your own, a unique and special design, that I want you to experience. Most of all, I want you to have fun creating your own piece of art in a vase.

two

VERSATILE VASES

CONTAINERS ARE AN INTEGRAL PART OF ANY ARRANGEMENT
AND SHOULD NEVER BE CONSIDERED AS AN AFTER-THOUGHT. IN
THE EXCITEMENT OF STARTING AN ARRANGEMENT IT IS EASY TO
OVERLOOK THE IMPORTANCE OF CHOOSING THE RIGHT VASE OR
POT, YET THE MOST DAZZLING ARRAY OF FLOWERS WILL JUST
NOT LOOK RIGHT IF THE WRONG CONTAINER IS USED. IDEALLY,
THE VESSEL AND THE FLOWERS SHOULD LOOK AS THOUGH THEY
WERE JUST MEANT TO BE TOGETHER, A PERFECT MATCH, ONE
COMPLEMENTING THE OTHER.

CONTAINERS FOR FLOWER ARRANGING COME IN MANY GUISES.
VASES AND JUGS ARE AN OBVIOUS STARTING POINT BUT IT IS
SURPRISING WHAT OTHER WATER-TIGHT VESSELS CAN BE USED.
GALVANIZED BUCKETS, OLD WEATHERED FLOWERPOTS, OLD
BOTTLES, WOODEN CRATES, KITCHENWARE, ALL CAN BE USED
TO GREAT EFFECT WITH A LITTLE IMAGINATION.

jug of flowers

1. 1 bunch Eucalyptus (*Eucalyptus* sp.)
2. 4 stems *Bupleurum griffithii*
3. 3 stems *Limonium emille*
4. 3 stems *Viburnum opulus*
5. 10 stems Ranunculus (*Ranunculus asiaticus*)
6. 5 Mini Gerbera 'Sardana' (*Gerbera* sp.)

A jug is ideal for an informal display of flowers. A simple yet appealing arrangement can be achieved easily, with very little effort. Try to link the jug and flowers together through the color scheme or style of arrangement. Here for example, a contemporary pattern on the china blends perfectly with the casual style of arrangement, and the bold use of shocking pink, fresh lime and lavender blue add to the modern informal look.

Difficulty: Easy

METHOD

1 Fill the jug approximately three quarters full with water. Remove any leaves which will fall below the water line from the flower and foliage stems, to prevent water pollution. Use a knife to cut all the stem ends diagonally. Start by arranging the eucalyptus at differing heights and widths to form a loose outline.

2 Add the bupleurum between the eucalyptus stems to provide a framework and support for the flowers.

OTHER MATERIALS

Jug, approx 8 inches high

3 Fill in between the bupleurum and eucalyptus with limonium, placing it throughout for an even distribution of color.

5 Finish the arrangement by adding ranunculus at various heights. Make sure every stem is inserted into the jug well below the water line, to ensure the arrangement lasts as long as possible. Top the water up every day.

The art in this type of arrangement is to create a loose, free style which is not too formal. In the finished arrangement the bold colors and natural style complement the jug perfectly.

4 Add the viburnum and gerbera next; these will give visual weight and focal areas to the design. Recess some pieces of viburnum to achieve depth within the arrangement.

1. 8 Iris 'Apollo' (*Iris sp.*)
2. 15 Narcissi 'Yellow Cheerfulness' (*Narcissus sp.*)
3. 6 Hyacinth 'City of Haarlem' (*Hyacinthus sp.*)
4. 15 Ranunculus (*Ranunculus asiaticus*)

1   2

3   4

OTHER MATERIALS

Old crate or wooden tray approx 12 x 13 inches
Plastic sheeting
8 Birch twigs (*Betula* sp.)
Floral foam
Sinamay, or similar open weave ribbon
Moss

spring meadow

The freshness of a spring meadow is caught perfectly in this design – you can almost feel a soft breeze blowing gently through the early flowers. To fit the mood of the arrangement, an old crate is used as the container. The flowers are used in bands of variety and color to give a tiered effect, bringing a country style right up to date.

Difficulty: Intermediate

METHOD

1 Line the crate with plastic sheeting and fill snugly with wet foam. Use moss to fill in the gaps in the crate. First use the tallest birch twigs, inserting them into the back of the foam. The tallest twigs are approximately twice the height of the container. Add more twigs to the middle and front of the foam, gradually reducing the length of stem, using the shortest twigs at the front of the crate.

2 As the tallest flowers, the iris are added in a line at the back of the arrangement. Cut the stem ends diagonally with a knife for easy insertion into the foam. Hold each stem straight above the arrangement and drop it through the birch twigs. Gently hold the stem base, and push into the foam. Shorten the second line of iris slightly.

5 At the front of the crate the hyacinth are added, with a few ranunculus placed low into the foam to bring the orange color down to the base of the arrangement. Finish off the design by covering the foam with moss, and tying the ribbon around the crate to break up the solid appearance of the container.

Use this style of arrangement with summer flowers to create an herbaceous border effect, or with reeds, bulrushes, and iris, covering the base with pebbles for a water garden.

3 Next, group the ranunculus in a line across the arrangement, reducing the stem lengths to produce a gradual step down.

This type of arrangement can be made in a variety of containers from seed trays and baking dishes, to old garden pots. Use your imagination to choose a container with character, but always make sure you use a waterproof liner inside the container.

4 Add the narcissi in front of the ranunculus, again reducing the length of stem to give a tiered effect.

Bringing a spring meadow indoors is easy to achieve by using this parallel style of arrangement, and the fragrance of the flowers will fill the room with the scents of spring.

"...Sweet good-night!
This bud of love, by Summer's ripening breath,
May prove a beauteous flower when next we meet."

WILLIAM SHAKESPEARE (1564 - 1616), *ROMEO AND JULIET*

sunshades

Terracotta pots make versatile and inexpensive containers for flower arrangements. The natural coloring and variety of shapes available makes it possible to find a pot suitable for any style of design. Old pots weathered with age are wonderful for natural country arrangements, while clean, simple-shaped containers lend themselves to modern and abstract designs. Here, the color of the pot is a perfect match for the peachy shades of amaryllis. The large anthurium leaves provide sunshades for the flowers, giving the whole design a tropical feel.

Difficulty: Intermediate

FLOWERS

1. 3 Amaryllis (*Hippeastrum* sp.)
2. 3 Anthurium leaves (*Anthurium* sp.)
3. 3 Typha leaves (*Liriope muscari*)
4. 5 Galax leaves (*Galax viceolata*)
5. 2 Aspidistra leaves

1

2

3

4

5

OTHER MATERIALS

Terracotta pot, 13 inches high
Floral foam
Moss
Cane
Kabob sticks
Small phial
Raffia

METHOD

1 To give additional height to one of the anthurium leaves attach a water-holding phial to a cane as follows. Wrap two galax leaves neatly around the phial, securing with raffia. Then tie the leaf-wrapped phial to one end of the cane. Add water to the phial. Top up the water daily.

2 Soak the foam and fit tightly into the terracotta pot. Position the cane to one side at the back of the foam, then insert an anthurium leaf into the phial.

3 Add two more anthurium leaves, one to the left of the first leaf, the other low down, covering the foam. Make sure spaces are left between the leaves for the flowers.

4 Add the first amaryllis below the tallest leaf. Amaryllis have large hollow stems, which can be difficult to insert into the foam. To give additional support to the flower, place a kabob stick into the foam first; this will fit inside the hollow amaryllis stem. Push the amaryllis stem over the kabob stick and into the foam.

6 Choose the most open amaryllis for the final flower which should be placed low down, by the base leaf.

7 Finish the design by placing aspidistra and looped typha leaves to the left hand side to add balance and visual weight to the base of the arrangement. Loop the typha leaves by pushing the base into the foam, making a loop and pinning the tip in position. Cover any exposed foam with moss.

5 Put the second amaryllis underneath the leaf to the left, using the technique described in step four.

Any large leaf can be used as a sunshade. Monstera, hosta, aspidistra, or papyrus leaves will serve equally well.

This arrangement is an ideal start for the beginner as it has very few flower placements, but will train the eye to recognize proportion, scale and balance within a design.

summer in the city

Many modern city apartments have minimalist interiors, providing a calm uncluttered environment to live in amid the hustle and bustle of the city. Contemporary chic arrangements like the one here are ideal for such a setting. Clean lines coupled with the zingy colors of citrus fruits create a unique, up-to-the-minute look for smart town living.

Difficulty: Intermediate

FLOWERS

1. 4 Gerbera 'Sundance' (*Gerbera* sp.)
2. 1 Gerbera 'Clementine' (*Gerbera* sp.)
3. 5 *Craspedia*
4. Ivy (*Hedera helix*)
5. Ming fern (*Asparagus myriocladus*)
6. Bear grass (*Xerophyllum tenax*)

OTHER MATERIALS

2 small containers approx 4½ inches square
1 oblong dish approx 11 x 6½ inches
Floral foam
Floral tape
1 small orange (or tangerine)
1 lime
Toothpicks

METHOD

1 Fill the two small containers with wet foam cut to fit snugly into each container, with approximately 1 inch showing above the rim of the container. Secure the foam by wrapping a length of floral tape around each container. Place the containers into the oblong dish.

2 Add two gerbera to each container. In the first container the tallest gerbera should be at least twice the height of the oblong dish. The second gerbera is placed low down with the head almost resting on the foam. In the other container, the tallest gerbera should be slightly lower than that in the first container. Position the flowers to look at each other as though talking. The orange gerbera is of medium height and placed to act as a stepping stone between the tallest and lowest flower.

3 Add a final flower to the back of the second container at the base of the tall flower. Position the ivy leaves low on the foam to give visual weight to the base of the design and to cover the foam. Take three strands of bear grass, insert the bottom ends firmly into the foam at the base of the tallest flower. Tie the tips to the stem just beneath the flower head. Take another three strands, and in the same way make a loop attached to the second tallest flower. A third group of bear grass forms a loop linking the two groups of flowers from left to right across the center of the arrangement and is held in position with hairpins.

Summer in the city is epitomized in this arrangement with the use of zingy citrus colors, lemon, lime and orange coupled with the simple bold shapes of the gerbera to give a truly modern, town appeal.

4 Cut the lime and orange in half. Push a toothpick into the base of the fruit for easy insertion into the foam. Add the craspedia into the center of the arrangement, grouping from back to front. Next, position half of the orange at the front right-hand corner of the design, and the limes in the center. Using the minimum foliage necessary, cover any exposed foam with more ivy and ming fern. The beauty of this design is the uncluttered lines, so do not make any fussy placements of foliage. Add the final half of orange to the back left-hand corner, to balance the design.

the drawing room

FLOWERS

1. 10 Roses 'Nicole' (*Rosa* sp.)
2. 7 Peonies 'Sarah Bernhardt' (*Paeonia* sp.)
3. 6 Stocks (*Matthiola incana*)
4. 12 Sweet Peas (*Lathyrus odoratus*)
5. 6 Spirea (*Spiraea* sp.)
6. 2 Love Lies Bleeding (*Amaranthus caudatus*)
7. 7 Solomon's Seal (*Polygonatum* sp.)
8. 7 *Aglaonema Crispum*, 'Silver Queen'
9. 6 stems Hebe (*Hebe* sp.)
10. Eucalyptus 'Baby Blue' (*Eucalyptus* sp.)
11. Rosemary (*Rosmarinus officinalis*)

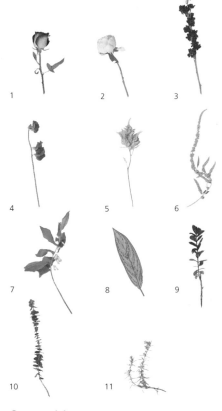

OTHER MATERIALS

Traditional pedestal container approx 8 x 11 inches
Floral foam
Floral tape

The container used will always suggest the most suitable style of arrangement. This is clearly shown in *The Drawing Room* where the container is a classic pedestal with traditional balustrade relief decoration. Old-fashioned summer flowers – peonies, sweet peas and stocks – tumble out in a riot of pink and burgundy shades, while the opulent cabbage roses are used to stunning effect in the center of the design. All are perfect accompaniments for a classic urn.

Difficulty: Hard

METHOD

1 Fill the container with wet floral foam. The foam should stand approximately one inch above the rim of the container. Secure the foam in the container with floral tape.

Depth is achieved in this arrangement by using materials at the front to fall over the edge of the container. These should be approximately one third the size of the tallest flower or foliage.

2 To form the outline, take a piece of eucalyptus and position in the center, toward the back of the foam. The eucalyptus should be at least twice the height of the container. Add Solomon's seal of approximately the same length to the sides of the foam at the back. These should drape over the rim of the container. To achieve depth, add an outline of foliage at the front, spilling out over the front of the container. Fill in the outline with more Solomon's seal, eucalyptus, rosemary, and silver queen leaves.

Large arrangements with a lot of flowers will need plenty of water. Make sure the container is deep enough to hold a reservoir of water. Top up with water daily.

3 Use the stocks and spirea as the tallest flowers; group some around the center back of the arrangement, use others to cascade over the edges at the side and front.

Larger leaves at the center of the arrangement will give visual weight to the focal area.

5 Add the roses through the center of the design, then along the bottom left, to form the focal area. Add the peonies to give visual weight to the focal area. Recess some of both flowers to give depth to the arrangement. Fill in where necessary with sweet peas, and finally add amaranthus in the center to fall over the front of the arrangement and trail onto the table.

4 Add sweet peas to the sides, placing them toward the back of the foam to create the widest part of the arrangement.

This is a traditional design with timeless appeal. The overall effect is high summer, with the blowsy roses and peonies cascading from the urn in a rich, luxurious riot of color.

C H A P T E R

three

C R Y S T A L   C L E A R

GLASS VASES ARE A NATURAL CHOICE FOR DISPLAYING FLOWERS
BECAUSE THEY REFLECT THE LIGHT, COLORS ARE ENHANCED AND
ANY FLOWER WILL BLEND PERFECTLY WITH THE CONTAINER. THE
WIDE VARIETY OF SHAPES AND STYLES AVAILABLE CAN BE
CONFUSING WHEN BUYING A GLASS VASE. LOOK FIRST AT WHERE
THE VASE IS TO BE PLACED, AS THIS WILL DETERMINE THE HEIGHT
AND   WIDTH   OF   THE   CONTAINER.   THEN   TAKE   INTO
CONSIDERATION THE ROOM AND STYLE OF DECOR.

COLORED GLASS NEEDS A LITTLE MORE THOUGHT PUT INTO THE
COLOR SCHEME BUT LOOKS STUNNING, PARTICULARLY WHEN
WELL LIT BY NATURAL OR ARTIFICIAL LIGHT. IT IS WISE TO
REMEMBER THAT THE WIDER THE NECK OF THE CONTAINER THE
MORE FLOWERS ARE NEEDED TO FILL IT. ALSO, THE STEMS OF THE
FLOWERS WILL BE SEEN AND PLAY AN IMPORTANT PART WITHIN
THE DESIGN SO SHOULD ALWAYS BE CLEAN AND NEAT.

floating flowers

In this arrangement, with one special stem of phalaenopsis orchid nestling on the pebbles, the swirling clematis encircling the bowl appears to cherish and protect these beautiful flowers, while the domed typha leaves cocoon the whole design. The pebbles anchor the flower stems into the bowl, which is then filled with water. This is an arrangement to look into, with the interest inside the bowl, making it ideal for a low coffee-table.

Difficulty: Intermediate

FLOWERS

1. *Clematis montana* 'Rubens'
2. 5 Typha leaves (*Liriope muscari*)
3. 1 stem Moth Orchid (*Phalaenopsis* sp.)

OTHER MATERIALS

Large glass bowl, 16 inches diameter
Pebbles
Clear sticky tape
Water

METHOD

1 Gently place a group of interesting shaped pebbles into the center of the bowl. Add the pebbles one at a time, building up the group until it is level with, or just below the rim of the bowl.

2 Take a long stem of clematis, push the stem end between the pebbles anchoring it securely. Then encircle the dish with the clematis, securing it to the rim of the dish with two small pieces of clear sticky tape.

3 Gently push the orchid stem between the pebbles resting the flower heads on the pebbles in the center of the bowl.

4 Make an arch of clematis to form a bridge above the bowl, again securing the stem end between the pebbles.

5 Take the typha leaves one at a time. Push the stem end between the stones, entwine around the clematis, twisting the grass for interest. Finish by anchoring the tip of the leaf between the group of pebbles.

6 When the canopy of typha grass is finished, tuck one or two clematis heads in among the pebbles. Add water to the bowl, covering the pebbles as far as possible, but making sure the heads of the orchid are just above the water line.

The dome of clematis and typha grass appears to lovingly protect and cosset the orchid, and draws the eye to its special beauty.

simplicity

FLOWERS

1. 6 stems Madonna Lilies (*Lilium longiflorum*)

2. Bear grass (*Xerophyllum tenax*)

1

2

OTHER MATERIALS

Glass vase approx 10 inches high
Twig ring approx 10 inches diameter
6 stems Twisted Willow (*Salix tortuosa*)
3 12 inch stub wires

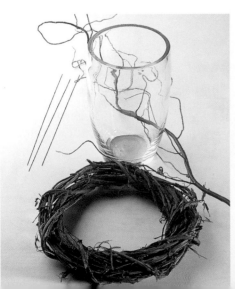

Some flowers are used to the best advantage in a simple design and this is definitely the case when using Madonna lilies. Their style and elegance needs to be shown alone and complicated designs will only detract from their fine shape. Here, the lilies are enhanced by the curving stems of willow, and with the addition of twigs inside the vase, interest is continued to the base of the design. These twigs also act as a support for the stems, keeping them in the required position.

Difficulty: Easy

METHOD

1 Cut off the smaller branches from the base of the willow and push them carefully into the vase to form a web to support the flower stems. Make sure the willow branches are evenly distributed to look interesting.

2 Take the twig ring, push a stub wire through the twigs, twist the wire together at the top, close to the twig ring, to form two legs. Make two more wire supports at equal distances around the ring.

3 Fit the twig ring around the top of the vase. Secure into place by attaching the wire legs to the twigs already inside the vase. Now fill the vase with water.

5 Cut the ends of the lily stems diagonally and remove any foliage which will fall below the water line. Arrange the lilies through the top branches and thread through the twigs in the base of the vase. The lilies will then stay in place. Cut the lily stems at differing heights for interest, with one or two stems shorter at the front of the arrangement. Add groups of bear grass to spill over the sides of the vase.

As the lilies open, remove the stamens to prevent the pollen marking clothes and furnishings.

4 Add the tall twisted willow twigs. These should be at least twice the height of the container. Arrange in the vase to create a natural support for the lilies.

Remember to change the water every few days to ensure the flowers last as long as possible.

The lily has always epitomized grace and elegance. Teamed with the simplicity of translucent glass, and brought up to date with the addition of twisted branches, this arrangement will happily fit into a traditional or modern setting.

"*...A lovelier flower*
On earth was never sewn..."

WILLIAM WORDSWORTH (1770 - 1850), *LUCY*

THIS ELEGANT GLASS VASE WITH ITS FLUID, CURVACACEOUS SHAPE IS SURROUNDED BY THE SHOOTING STAR EFFECT OF *GLORIOSA ROTHSCHILDIANA*

vibrance

FLOWERS

1. 4 Roses 'Ambience' (*Rosa* sp.)
2. 5 Mini Gerbera 'Paso' (*Gerbera* sp.)
3. 5 Marigolds (*Calendula officinalis*)
4. 5 Ranunculus (*Ranunculus asiaticus*)
5. 5 stems Spray Carnations (*Dianthus kortina*)
6. 4 stems Hypericum 'Excellent Flair' (*Hypericum* sp.)
7. 3 stems Spray Chrysanthemums 'Santini Kermit' (*Chrysanthemum* sp.)
8. 10 stems *Alchemilla mollis*
9. 4 Ming fern (*Asparagus myriocladus*)
10. 5 Leather leaf (*Arachniodes adiantiformis*)
11. 20 Bear grass (*Xerophyllum tenax*)

OTHER MATERIALS

Large , green glass vase 9 x 9 inches
Strong tying twine or raffia

Splash out and be adventurous with color; look around at the natural color schemes in plants and flowers for inspiration. Today's home furnishings can also give you ideas of how to combine exciting colors. The vibrant autumnal colors in this hand-tied bouquet complement the lime green glass vase perfectly. Do not be afraid to mix clashing colors; here rich reds, brilliant orange, and gold run riot with the shocking pink of the roses. Hand tying the flowers is simple once you master the basic technique and this style creates a winning 'just picked' bunch effect.

Difficulty: Hard

METHOD

1 Remove any foliage and thorns from the stems which will be below the tying point of the bouquet. Lay out all the flowers in groups on the table for easy access. Then take a small bunch of alchemilla and ming fern, hold in your hand where the tying point will be. Approximately eight inches of foliage should be above the hand for this bouquet. This foliage provides a support for the focal flowers. If right handed, hold the bouquet in the left hand and feed stems in with the right hand, and vice versa if left handed.

2 Insert a rose through the middle of the foliage first, then take one of each of the other flowers and group them around the rose. To achieve neat spiralling stems, place flowers and foliage from left to right at the front, and from right to left at the back of the bouquet.

3 Continue adding all the flowers in pleasing
patterns, evenly distributing the colors and with
foliage in between to create an open effect. Add
the bear grass in groups to give movement to the
design. Shorten the length of the outer flowers
to give a nice rounded profile to the bouquet.

5 The bouquet will stand on its own if the
stems are cut into an inverted 'V' shape at the
bottom. Cut the stems to a length to fit the vase.
Fill the vase with deep water, place the finished
bouquet in the vase.

4 Finish the bouquet with an edging of leather
leaf. The bouquet is now ready to tie in place.
Take a long length of twine or raffia and double
it. Pass it around the stems and pull the two ends
of the twine through the loop. Separate the ends
and pull firmly. Bind the twine around the stems
again, pulling tightly, and finish with a firm knot.

The finished effect of the autumnal colors is brilliance at its best. The color of the glass vase enhances the theme and combines with the loose, natural shape of the bouquet to produce a haze of floral glory.

blue bottles

FLOWERS

1. 3 stems Moth Orchids (*Phalaenopsis* sp.)

1

When you have only one or two exotic or special flowers, they need to be shown off to their full advantage. Here, a group of deep blue bottles clustered together combine with three stems of shocking pink moth orchids to give dramatic and immediate impact. The twisted willow adds movement and rhythm to the design, with the shimmering blue marbles at the base finishing the effect.

Difficulty: Easy

METHOD

1 Spray the twigs with paint to match the flowers. Before spraying, protect the work surface with an old newspaper and make sure the room is well ventilated. Always follow the manufacturer's instructions and observe safety precautions when spraying.

OTHER MATERIALS

Selection of bottles in varying sizes and shapes
Dish or tray 10 x 14 inches
Marbles
Stems of Twisted willow (*Salix tortuosa*)
Spray paint to match the color of the flowers

2 Group the bottles into the tray, placing smaller bottles to the front.

3 Add enough marbles to cover the base of the tray. These will help to keep the bottles securely in place.

5 Fill the bottles which will hold the flowers with water, add the longest stem of orchids to a bottle at the back of the tray, arching it high over the bottles. Finish the arrangement by adding a stem of orchids to a shorter bottle at the front. Fill the tray with water, then add the final orchid, pushing the stem between the marbles.

4 Allow the paint to dry on the twigs then add the tallest twig to one of the bottles at the back. The other twig is secured in the marbles at the base, and threaded through the bottles to the other side of the tray.

This beautiful orchid is both impressive and dramatic. The color of the bottles is a perfect foil, and the simplicity of this arrangement shows the orchid stems off to their very best.

Silver sand, pebbles or moss can be used in the base dish instead of marbles.

Lines and groups of bottles along a mantel shelf also make an interesting display when a few dramatic flowers are added.

dancing stems

The willowy stem of a tulip has a beauty all of its own; it bends and curves in the most graceful way if left to its own devices. One of the reasons for this is because the stem keeps on growing when cut and placed in water. *Dancing Stems* makes the most of this natural grace, the parrot tulips with their irregular-shaped petals and striking color stand alone except for loops of grass. To accentuate the color harmony, the water is tinted to match the tulips.

Difficulty: Easy

FLOWERS

1. 11 Parrot Tulips, 'Estella Rijnveld' (*Tulipa* sp.)
2. Typha leaves (*Liriope muscari*)

OTHER MATERIALS

4 clear glass vases in a variety of shapes and heights
Food coloring to match the flower color
Clear sticky tape
Water

METHOD

1 Add a few drops of food coloring to a jug of water, stir and then fill the specimen vases to different heights with the colored water.

2 Position the vases in an interesting group with the tallest to the back. Add three tulips to the tallest vase, and three tulips to the shortest vase, all with differing stem lengths. Choose and position each tulip so that it curves naturally in the desired direction.

Sometimes it is difficult to keep the flowers in place in wider necked vases. Cellophane crunched up or shredded, then pushed into the base of the vase will hold the stems in place.

4 Add three typha leaves between the vases to link each container together. One piece is tied around the neck of a tulip for added interest.

3 Add three tulips to each of the remaining vases. If the neck of the vase is wide and the tulips will not stand still in their position, take a small amount of clear sticky tape and make a grid over the top of the vase, securing the tape on either side of the vase. This will form transparent criss-crosses which will keep the stems in place.

Coloring the water in vases is easy and fun to do. It is not harmful to the flowers, and they will not change color, as the food coloring is diluted with water.

Simple to achieve, this group of arrangements will give endless pleasure as you watch the tulip stems twist and turn, changing shape constantly.

four

MAGICAL METALS

THE SHIMMER AND SHINE OF METALS CAN BE A MAGICAL ADDITION TO A FLOWER ARRANGEMENT. THE LUSTER OF GOLD AND BRONZE BRINGS OPULENCE AND LUXURY TO A DESIGN, WHILE SILVER SUGGESTS GRACIOUS LIVING. HOWEVER CONTAINERS DO NOT HAVE TO BE COLLECTORS' PIECES. OLD GALVANIZED BUCKETS, WATERING CANS, BOWLS OF ALL DESCRIPTIONS MAKE WONDERFUL RECEPTACLES FOR NATURAL STYLES OF ARRANGEMENT — A BIT OF RUST OR DIRT ONLY ADDS TO THEIR ATTRACTION. LOOK OUT FOR OLD TEA CHESTS, CADDIES AND CANNISTERS — ALL CAN HAVE THEIR MOMENT OF GLORY AS TREASURE CHESTS FULL OF FLOWERS. THIS CHAPTER SHOWS HOW DIVERSE THE RANGE OF STYLES CAN BE USING METALS AS THE BASIS FOR DESIGN.

elegance

FLOWERS

1. 4 stems Lilies (*Lilium pompeii*)
2. Blue Fir (*Picea pungens*)
3. Japanese Anemone leaves (*Anemone hupehensis*)
4. Rosemary (*Rosmarinus officialis*)
5. Typha leaves (*Liriope muscari*)

1   2

3   4

5

OTHER MATERIALS

Metal candlestick 22 inches high
3 18 inch church candles
Floral foam
Floral tape
2 small plastic foam holders
Fixing tape

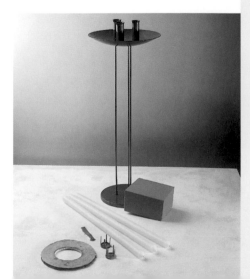

A green and white color scheme is guaranteed to create an elegant look and this certainly is the case with this graceful design. The creamy-white lilies are set off to perfection by the shades of green, and the variegated foliage add texture and shape to the design. This floor-standing arrangement will bring a touch of sophistication to any special occasion.

Difficulty: Intermediate

METHOD

1 Place the three candles into the holders. Attach the two plastic foam holders to the metal dish with fixing tape. Cut two pieces of wet foam to fit into the metal dish. Push these onto the foam holders and secure with floral tape across both pieces of foam, anchoring the tape to the underside of the dish.

2 Select pieces of foliage with a natural cascading shape, that will flow down over the rim of the dish. Clean the lower part of the stems to insert into the side of the foam. Use blue fir on one side then trail rosemary on the other side. Then add typha leaves, arranging them to flow over the front and back. Add Japanese anemone leaves, inserting the stems into the side of the foam.

3 Place the open lilies in the center of the arrangement, low into the design, grouping them all around the candles to give focal areas.

4 The lily buds are used to make a graceful line, with one stem falling over the side of the dish, the other stem placed to stand straight, near the candles on the opposite side. Finish with loops of typha leaves: push one stem into the foam, curve the leaf to form a loop and then push the other end of the leaf into the foam or pin in place with hairpins.

This stunning, elegant arrangement is a classic style which will grace the most formal occasion.

Candles can be a fire hazard. Never leave lit candles unattended. Keep materials well away from naked flames.

jewels

FLOWERS

1. 15 Roses 'Souvenir' (*Rosa* sp.)
2. 20 Anemones 'Mona Lisa blue' (*Anemone* sp.)
3. 20 Sweet Peas, pale and dark pink (*Lathyrus odoratus*)
4. *Senecio greyii*
5. Eucalyptus 'Baby Blue' (*Eucalyptus* sp.)
6. 5 Kochia (*Maireana sedifolia*)
7. Bear grass (*Xerophyllum tenax*)

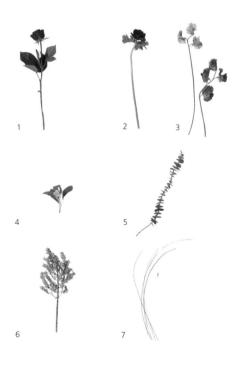

OTHER MATERIALS

Galvanized container approx 10 inch diameter
Floral foam
Wire hairpin

The rich colors of bygone days produce a dramatic jewel effect in this low arrangement suitable for a dinner-table or low coffee-table. It's an arrangement to look into, with strong groups of roses, anemones and sweet peas complemented by the gray foliage of kochia, senecio, and eucalyptus, styled in a galvanized container to reflect the color scheme. When using metal containers make sure they are watertight, otherwise use a plastic liner or dish inside the container. Always place the finished arrangement on a mat to protect the table underneath.

Difficulty: Intermediate

METHOD

1 Fill the container snugly with floral foam. Make sure the foam is approximately one inch above the rim of the container.

2 Add the foliage around the edges and into the center of the foam, making large groups of senecio, kochia, and eucalyptus. Keep all the foliage short, approximately six inches in length. Make sure the handles of the container are not covered by foliage.

3 Between the foliage, make groups of three to five roses to create strong blocks of color. Do the same with the anemones. Keep all the flowers the same height, approximately six inches.

4 Add the sweet peas between the groups of anemones and roses, making sure the sections of gray foliage are still visible. Bring some of the sweet peas down at the sides to give a slightly domed effect. Divide the bear grass into two. Insert stems into the foam at either side of the design, form two loops over the arrangement and bring all the grass together at the center front. Hold in place with a hairpin. Add a few strands of grass to fall over the edge of the container at the front.

This arrangement conjures up images of a bygone age, with old-fashioned flowers in an array of rich jewel-like colors. Yet the theme is brought up to date by using strong placements of flowers complemented by the subtle grays of the foliage.

"*From the soft wing of vernal breezes shed,*
Anemonies; auriculas, enriched
With shining meal o'er all their velvet leaves;
And full ranunculas, of glowing red."

A.C. SWINBURNE (1837 - 1909), *ATALANTA IN CALYDON*

gilt edged

FLOWERS

1. 4 Gerbera 'Darling' (*Gerbera* sp.)
2. 4 Roses 'Cream Prohyta' (*Rosa* sp.)
3. 5 stems Lizianthus (*Eustoma russellianum*)
4. 3 stems Hypericum 'Excellent Flair' (*Hypericum* sp.)
5. 4 Aspidistra leaves (*Gerbera* sp.)
6. 7 Galax leaves (*Galax Viceolata*)
7. Eucalyptus (*Eucalyptus* sp.)
8. Bear grass (*Xerophyllum tenax*)
9. Leather leaf (*Arachniodes adiantiformis*)
10. Ming fern (*Asparagus umbellatus*)

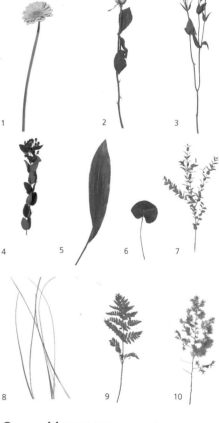

OTHER MATERIALS

Deep glass fruit bowl,   Moss
   9 inches diameter   Bullion, gold metal thread
Floral foam   Gold spray paint
Wires for hairpins   Gold bauble

An aureole of flowers surrounds a shimmering glass bauble in this fabulous centerpiece for a special occasion. Using soft shades of peach and cream flowers, the foliage is dusted with gold to emphasize the glowing champagne tones of the bauble, while a cobweb of metallic wire adds the finishing touch, catching the light to create a flickering meshwork over the whole arrangement.

Difficulty: Intermediate

METHOD

1 Protect the work surface with newspaper then spray the bear grass with gold paint. Work in a well-ventilated room and follow the manufacturer's instructions carefully.

2 Line the bowl with damp moss to provide an attractive finish and hide the floral foam.

3 Fit the floral foam snugly into the bowl, inside the moss layer. Scoop out a hollow in the center of the foam to form a resting place for the gold bauble.

4 Place the bauble into the hollow made in the foam.

5 Add the eucalyptus and leather leaf to form a circle of foliage around the bauble, bringing it out over the rim of the bowl.

7 Insert the gerbera into the foam around the bauble at equal distances, to achieve a good balance of color.

6 Give the aspidistra leaves a light dusting of gold spray paint. When dry, insert a stem into the foam, then twist the leaf to form a loop and secure the tip of the leaf into the foam with a hairpin. Do the same with two or three more leaves. Fill in around the edge with galax leaves.

8 Place the roses between the gerbera, then fill in with lizianthus around the edges and into the center between the other flowers.

9 Divide the bear grass into small groups. Take each group and insert the stem ends into the foam, make loops then use a hairpin to secure the tips of the grass into the foam. Finally, pull out the strand of bullion and thread this around and over all the flowers to create a fine cobweb.

The lustrous effect of the bauble combined with the halo of flowers forms a chic arrangement ideal for a candlelit dinner party or a special celebration meal.

a bowl of sunshine

FLOWERS

1. 15 Aspidistra leaves
2. 10 Sunflowers (*Helianthus annuus*)
3. Bear grass (*Xerophyllum tenax*)

We don't always have the right container for the arrangement we want to make, but with a little ingenuity, plastic pots or old containers can be given a new lease of life by wrapping them with leaves. An old plastic container is disguised in just this way for this bowl of sunflowers. These wonderful flowers have such impact that they are usually best used alone, but in this case aspidistra leaves are curled to produce a wavy sea of greenery which acts as a perfect foil to the sunflowers.

Difficulty: Intermediate

METHOD

1 Place a piece of double-sided sticky tape on either end of the aspidistra leaves.

OTHER MATERIALS

Large plastic bowl, 10 inches diameter
Block of floral foam
Double-sided sticky tape
Stapler and staples

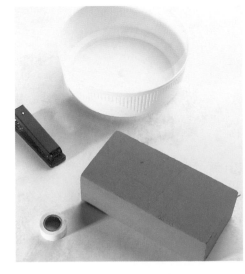

2 Stick the leaves to the outside of the bowl, overlapping each one to completely cover the bowl and give a neat finish.

3 Add wet foam to the bowl, cutting it to fit neatly. The foam should be just below the rim of the bowl. Take each remaining aspidistra leaf, curl the tip and staple the tip and leaf together inside the curl. The staples should not be visible.

5 Take one tall sunflower and insert it into the center of the foam. Add four more sunflowers around this central flower to form a tree effect. Tie the sunflowers together just below the heads with bear grass.

4 Once curled, insert the aspidistra leaves into the foam to form a bouncing collar around the edge of the bowl.

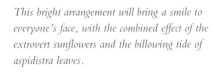

6 Insert the remaining sunflowers low down on the foam at the base of the tree.

This bright arrangement will bring a smile to everyone's face, with the combined effect of the extrovert sunflowers and the billowing tide of aspidistra leaves.

"The pansy at my feet
Doth the same tale repeat:
Whither is fled the visionary gleam?
Where is the now, the glory and the dream?"

WILLIAM WORDSWORTH (1770 - 1850), *ODE. INTIMATIONS OF IMMORTALITY*

networking

It is not often that the mechanics of an arrangement form part of the design, usually great care is taken to hide the method of construction. In this design, however, the wire mesh which supports the flowers forms an integral part of the design. The simple arrangement relies on bold flowers and leaves to make a long lasting floral statement. Perhaps this design will suggest to you other ways of using a support as a design element.

Difficulty: Easy

FLOWERS

1. 3 stems Lily 'Rosatto' (*Lilium* sp.)
2. 2 *Calathea insignis* leaves
3. 2 *Dracena* leaves (*Dracena* sp.)
4. Bear grass (*Xerophyllum tenax*)

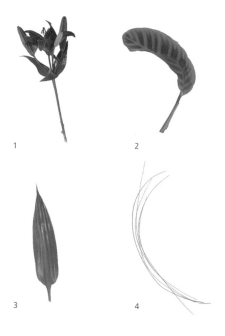

1

2

3

4

OTHER MATERIALS

Large shallow glass bowl appprox 22 inch diameter
6–8 small pebbles
Wire mesh 24 x 7 inches

Groups of pebbles are ideal for anchoring stems into glass bowls. A pin holder can be used under the stones for extra support if desired.

METHOD

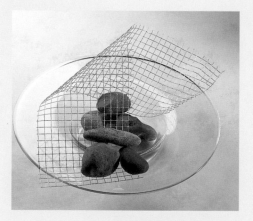

1 Using the glass bowl as a guide, twist the mesh to form an interesting curve over the bowl, with the ends of the mesh flattened slightly at the edges (the wire mesh will bend easily). Place pebbles on the flattened end of mesh at the front to anchor it in position. Place one or two more pebbles into the well of the bowl; these pebbles will help to keep the stems in place.

2 Cut one of the lily stems, and push it through the mesh into the well of the bowl. The lily heads should almost rest on the wire mesh. The mesh will hold the lily heads in place, while the stones at the base will keep the stem firmly anchored.

5 Add the two dracena leaves to the opposite side to the calathea leaves, to give the design visual balance. Again these leaves should rest on the edges of the glass bowl with the stems tucked between the pebbles. To complete the arrangement, add the bear grass to the front, anchoring the ends in the pebbles. Finally pour water into the well of the bowl, and top up daily.

3 Add the other two lily stems. Put one at the front of the arrangement below the height of the first stem, again pushing the stem through the wire mesh for anchorage. Put the remaining lily to the side of the arrangement at a lower level, with the stem pushed between the stones.

4 Add two calathea leaves to one side of the dish, resting them on the rim of the glass bowl with the stems pushed into the well of the container. Push the ends of the stems between the pebbles for anchorage.

Very few flowers are needed in this arrangement to create a design with maximum impact. Remember that the wire mesh is an important part of the design and should not be hidden.

five

FABULOUS FOLIAGE

VERY RARELY IN NATURE DO YOU SEE FLOWERS ON THEIR OWN WITHOUT A BACKDROP OF FOLIAGE. GREENERY HAS A CALMING EFFECT AND WHEN PLACED WITH ANY COLOR FLOWERS IT SKILLFULLY HELPS TO BLEND THE SHADES AND TONES TOGETHER. THE IMPORTANCE OF FOLIAGE IN FLORAL ART CANNOT BE EMPHASIZED ENOUGH; WITHOUT IT FLOWERS CAN LOOK STARK, BARE AND UNNATURAL. FOLIAGE ALSO GIVES VISUAL WEIGHT TO THE BASE OF DESIGNS.

FABULOUS FOLIAGE CAN CREATE WONDERFUL ARRANGEMENTS IN ITS OWN RIGHT. THERE ARE INFINITE PERMUTATIONS OF COLOR, SHAPE, AND TEXTURE TO CHOOSE FROM. THIS CHAPTER IS DEVOTED TO FOLIAGE SHOWING NEW LOOKS WITH TIMELESS APPEAL, AND GIVING GREENERY ITS RIGHTFUL ACCOLADE.

dreaming spires

FLOWERS

1. 5 Papyrus (*Cyperus papyrus*)
2. 6 Snake Grass (*Equisetum* sp.)
3. 3 stems Spray Chrysanthemums, 'Revert' (*Chrysanthemum* sp.)
4. 10 *Craspedia*
5. 20 Galax leaves (*Galax*)
6. 5 Croton leaves (*Codiaeum* sp.)
7. Ming fern (*Asparagus myriocladus*)

1   2

3   4   5

6   7

OTHER MATERIALS

Large shallow dish, 20 inches diameter
Floral foam
Raffia
7-inch stub wire

Rising from the undergrowth, dreaming spires of papyrus reach for the sky, looking like temples of some long-forgotten tribe. The base of the arrangement is textured with a variety of foliage and highlighted with the yellow craspedia to link the container and arrangement together. Snake grass draws the eye to the finials, making them the focal point to the design.

Difficulty: Intermediate

METHOD

1 Take three of the papyrus brushes and tie each of the grass heads neatly together toward the top of the brush, to form the spires.

🌿

This arrangement is a form of parallel design. It is one of the simplest styles to master. In a true parallel arrangement all the flowers are placed in clusters, vertically parallel to each other.

2 Pack the container with wet floral foam. The foam should rise approximately half an inch above the height of the container. Cut the three papyrus stems to varying heights, the tallest at least twice the length of the container. It is the height of the spires that adds the drama to this design, so keep the papyrus tall. Push the three spires into the foam slightly off center, toward the back. Cut the remaining two papyrus right down, so that the heads rest on the foam when the stems are pushed into it. These heads are the start of the textured base.

4 Now add in the base color with craspedia, croton leaves and chrysanthemum. All these items are used low, mainly resting on the foam again, to make interesting patterns and shapes whilst hiding the foam. Make sure all the foam is covered. Finally, add the snake grass in three groups of two stems. Position the two outer groups first; insert the stem ends into the foam, angle the stems diagonally outward, then bend the top of the grass to point inward. Put the third group of snake grass in front of the tallest spire, leave the tops straight but cut them to about two thirds the length of the spire. This will strengthen and emphasize the strong lines.

3 Take the stems cut from the papyrus and lie them across the top of the foam, to make an interesting pathway through the foliage. Bend a seven-inch stub wire to form a hairpin. Push the hairpin over the stems and into the foam to keep them in place. Add groups of galax leaves and ming fern to cover the foam and give interest to the base. The foliage should come over the edge of the container, in irregular patterns. Use contrasting textures as neighbors, for example a group of galax leaves next to ming fern.

The tall parallels generally rise from a textured base. This is achieved by placing foliage, moss, seed heads, fabric or flowers in groups, low onto the foam. By overlapping leaves, terracing flowers, or clustering berries together interesting patterns and textures are formed over the base. This type of textured arrangement can also look super on its own, placed on a low coffee-table so that the shapes and pathways can be seen clearly.

Parallel designs are best made in shallow containers with flat bases. Try a window-box style using a long shallow container and placing groups of straight flowers along its length.

This type of arrangement is very long-lasting. The papyrus and snake grass will dry off naturally. Keep replacing any wilted flowers or leaves at the base. Remember to keep the foam moist.

fragrance

FLOWERS

1. 20 stems Lily of the Valley (*Convallaria majalis*)
2. 1 large Anthurium leaf
3. Moss

1

2

3

Lily of the valley has such a short flowering season that it must be captured and enjoyed indoors as quickly as possible. The luxury of lily of the valley is its delicate silhouette and exquisite scent, which will fill a room with sweet perfume. Here the flowers are cocooned within a single leaf which has been cut to decorate a plain kitchen bowl.

Difficulty: Easy

METHOD

Foliage must be conditioned well to ensure a long life. Some leaves benefit from being submerged in water before use. All foliage should have a long drink before use.

1 Push the foam holder firmly onto the bottom of the glass bowl, making sure the holder is in the middle. Stick double-sided sticky tape around the outside of the bowl, approximately half an inch from the top.

OTHER MATERIALS

Small glass bowl, 9 inch diameter
Small foam holder with sticky floral fix on base
Double-sided sticky tape
Raffia
Small piece of foam

Many types of leaf can be used to cover unsightly or old containers. Choose a leaf which is strong and will not wilt rapidly. Thick, fleshy leaves such as laurel or ivy are best.

2 Cut the anthurium leaf into six pieces. These pieces will cover the outside of the bowl and line the inside also.

6 Continue the natural look by adding foliage and covering the foam at the base with moss.

5 Insert the lily of the valley into the foam in a natural way, to make it look as though it is growing in the container.

3 Take three of the pieces and wrap them around the outside of the bowl to completely cover it. The leaves should stick firmly to the double-sided tape. Once the leaves are in place, tie with raffia.

4 Line the inside of the bowl with the remaining two pieces of leaf. Push a piece of wet foam onto the foam holder. The foam will help to hold the leaf pieces in place.

Make a long, diagonal cut at the stem end to enable maximum water intake.

The pretty nodding bells of the lily of the valley are a traditional flower for brides' bouquets. Here it is used at its best, in a simple way, capturing the fragrance of springtime.

*"For winter's rains and ruins are over,
And all the season of snows and sins;
The days dividing lover and lover,
The light that loses, the night that wins;
And time remembered is grief forgotten,
And frosts are slain and flowers begotten,
And in green underwood and cover
Blossom by blossom the spring begins."*

A.C. SWINBURNE (1837 - 1909), *ATALANTA IN CALYDON*

verdant palettes

FLOWERS

1. 4 Anthurium 'Midori' (*Anthurium* sp.)
2. 3 *Mollucella laevis*
3. 4 Love Lies Bleeding (*Amaranthus caudatus*)
4. 6 stems *Viburnum opulus*
5. Ming fern (*Asparagus myriocladus*)
6. Ivy (*Hedera helix*)

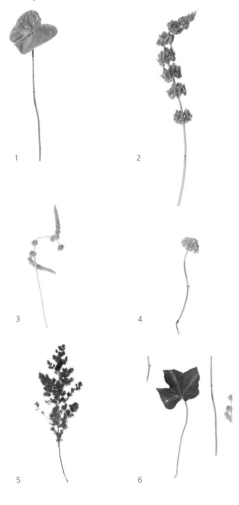

1   2

3   4

5   6

OTHER MATERIALS

Foam wreath ring with plastic holder, 12 inches diameter
10-inch stub wires
Raffia

Here, a wreath of foliage is encircled by the swirling stems of the anthuriums. Commonly called painter's palette, these remarkable flowers have pliable stems which, if gently manipulated, will curve gracefully to form patterns. The base of the arrangement is textured with a variety of green foliage and flowers to produce an oasis of calm, drifting greenery.

Difficulty: Hard

METHOD

1   Trim the edges of the foam ring with a knife to give a rounded shape. Take the foam ring to the sink, submerge in water for a few minutes only, then drain off excess water.

2   Arrange three groups of ivy leaves around the ring. Angle the leaves on the outer edge down to touch the table top, keep other leaves flat across the top, and angle leaves on the inner edge down over the foam. The hole in the center of the ring should be visible when finished.

Most foliage will benefit from being submerged in water for about half an hour. Gray foliage is the exception, this will lose its gray color if submerged.

3 Add the viburnum close to the ivy in four groups, the heads should rest on the foam with the stems pushed well in to get maximum water.

5 Place these groups of florets in patterns between the viburnum and ivy, with amaranthus grouped to trail out at the sides of the ring. Make sure the hole in the center of the wreath is still visible.

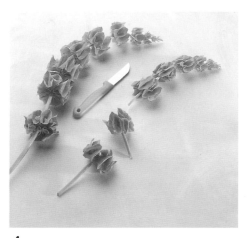

4 Cut the mollucella just above each group of florets, all the way up the stem to give small pieces of flower.

To get the maximum life from foliage it should be treated with as much care as flowers.

6 Fill in any gaps with ming fern. The whole of the wreath base should now be covered with interesting textures and shades of green.

7 Make four long hairpins with the stub wires. Insert the anthurium stems firmly into the foam, then gently stroke and bend the stems to swirl around the base. By gently manipulating the stem it will curve easily, if you are too forceful it will snap off. To keep the anthurium heads in position, put a hairpin over the stem just below the head, then push the hairpin into the foam.

Use foliage as design elements, not just to cover the foam. Think about how to use it to its full potential.

The luminous color of the anthurium is complemented by the shades of green in the textured base, giving a lush tropical effect.

the conservatory

FLOWERS

1. 2 stems *Mollucella laevis*
2. 2 stems Love Lies Bleeding (*Amaranthus caudatus*)
3. 5 stems *Viburnum opulus*
4. 5 Cycas leaves (*Cycas revoluta*)
5. 3 stems Spray Chrysanthemums, 'Revert'
   (*Chrysanthemum* sp.)
6. 4 small Palm leaves (*Chamaedorea elegans*)
7. 4 *Calathea insignis* leaves
8. Philodendron leaves (*Philodendron* sp.)

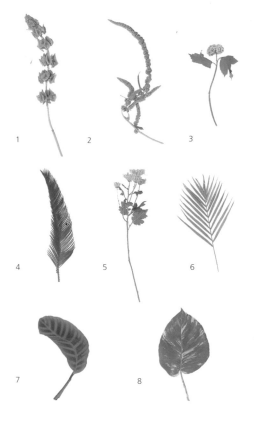

OTHER MATERIALS

Cast iron garden urn approx 10 inches diameter
Plastic dish or liner to fit inside urn
Floral foam
Floral tape
Small cabbage
3 Kabob sticks

Learning to value foliage is an important part of becoming an expert flower arranger. Here, an all green arrangement provides another option on a classical theme. Using an iron garden urn and a variety of lovely foliage it shows the diversity of foliage and the beauty of greenery used on its own. To make monochromatic color schemes work, the secret is to choose a variety of differing textures as this will draw the eye from one area of the arrangement to another.

Difficulty: Hard

METHOD

1 Fill the plastic dish with wet floral foam, the foam should stand at least one inch above the rim of the dish. Secure the foam in place with floral tape. When using the floral tape, take it over the top of the foam and secure to either side of the dish. Ensure the dish is completely dry otherwise the tape will not stick to it. Place the liner inside the urn.

2 Start by adding the two stems of mollucella to the center back of the foam. These should be approximately twice the height of the container. Add the palm leaves to both sides of the urn to flow over the sides of the container. Then put one cycas leaf to one side of the mollucella, and the philodendron leaves at the front of the foam and behind the mollucella.

Place foliage in a
bucket of water and
give it a long drink
before use. Once cut
never leave out of
water.

3 Add another cycas leaf to the one already at
the back of the arrangement, cutting the second
one slightly shorter. Twist the other cycas leaf to
form a loop, use a stub wire to bind the ends
together and place to fall over the front of the
arrangement. Add the viburnum, grouped from
left to right through the center of the design.
Peel off any unsightly outer leaves on the
cabbage and cut the end into a point. Take three
kabob sticks and push them firmly into the
cabbage at different angles.

*The ideal time to pick
garden foliage is first
thing in the morning,
when the dew is still
on the ground and the
foliage has had rest
and been replenished
with water. Never cut
foliage in the midday
heat, it will wilt
rapidly.*

*When cutting foliage
use a knife, and cut
the stem end
diagonally to expose
as much of the water-
carrying cell structure
inside the stem as
possible.*

4 Push the cabbage firmly into the center of
the arrangement. Use the spray chrysanthemums
to fill in any gaps and cover the foam. Finally,
add the amaranthus, trailing it out of the center
and side of the design. The leaves in the
arrangement will benefit from daily spraying
with water.

Large, round leaves are essential at the base of any design to give visual weight and draw the eye right down to the foot of the arrangement.

This arrangement is both lush and restful, perfect for formal entertaining when a grand statement must be made to impress.

six

F R U I T S & F L O W E R S

A RICH HARVEST OF DESIGNS CAN BE MADE INCORPORATING

FRUITS, BERRIES AND VEGETABLES. THEY CAN HELP TO MAKE THE

PERFECT ARRANGEMENT FOR THE DINING-ROOM OR KITCHEN,

THEIR TEXTURES AND SHAPES BRINGING IN NEW DESIGN

ELEMENTS. WE TEND TO THINK OF THESE TYPES OF ARRANGE-

MENTS AS SPECIFICALLY FOR FALL AND WINTER, BUT IN SPRING

AND SUMMER THERE IS ALWAYS AN ABUNDANCE OF PRODUCE

TO CHOOSE FROM. THE SUPERB RANGE OF COLORS AVAILABLE

MEANS THAT ANY COLOR SCHEME CAN BE CREATED. DRIED

FRUITS ARE PERFECT FOR RUSTIC ARRANGEMENTS WHICH WILL

LAST AND LAST, WHILE FOR AN UP-TO-THE-MINUTE STYLE, THE

BRILLIANT COMBINATION OF ORANGES, LEMONS, AND LIMES

IS PERFECT.

fruit cocktail

FLOWERS

1. 20 stems Icelandic Poppies (*Papaver* sp.)

1

Good enough to eat, this scrumptious combination of fruits and flowers is perfect for a buffet or dining table. The bright colors of strawberries, limes, kumquats and tangerines are vividly echoed in the vigorous colors of the poppies. The poppies are held in place by threading the stems through a twig ball, with their nodding heads twisting in different directions to give rhythm and movement to the design.
Difficulty: Easy

METHOD

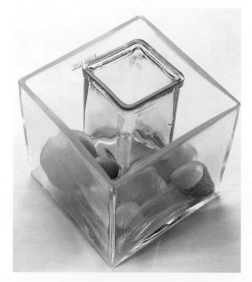

1 Place the smaller glass container tightly into one corner of the other container. Start to fill in the gap between the containers with fruit.

OTHER MATERIALS

1 square glass container, 6 inches diameter
1 square glass container, 3 inches diameter
1 twig ball
10 kumquats
6 strawberries
3 limes
2 tangerines
Adhesive tape (optional)

2 Pile up the fruits so that the colors are evenly distributed, and the space between the containers is completely filled.

5 Graduate the length of the stems at the front, using more open and shorter flowers to give a focal point, and evenly distributing the colors to harmonize with the fruits.

3 Fill the small container with water. Place the twig ball (see page 25) over the top, and if necessary secure the ball to the outer glass container with adhesive tape.

4 Starting with the tallest poppies, thread the stems of the flowers through the twig ball and into the water in the container.

Designed to refresh the taste-buds and bring the sunshine into your dining-room, this arrangement is a recipe for success.

citrus grove

FLOWERS

1. 55 Lemons
2. 6 stems Salal (*Gaultheria shallon*)

1   2

When citrus fruits are plentiful, a "tree" made entirely of lemons can make a striking modern alternative to an arrangement. In this floor-standing tree, the sharp, tangy scent of lemons with their bright lime-yellow coloring contrasts with the deep blue container, giving it the fresh appeal of a citrus grove. Display the tree alone, or in pairs either side of an entrance or buffet table, where the dramatic size will have maximum impact.

Difficulty: Intermediate

METHOD

OTHER MATERIALS

Ceramic pot, 8 inches diameter
Plastic bucket to fit inside pot
22-inch birch (*Betula* sp.) or similar wood pole
Foam sphere, 10 inches diameter
Ready-mix cement
10-inch stub wires
4-inch green sticks, pointed at one end
Carpet moss (*Minum* sp.)

1 Cut a spearhead shape on the top of the birch stick with a saw. Following the manufacturer's instructions make up the cement. Add it to the plastic bucket then push the pole into the center of the cement. Make sure the pole is upright. Leave to dry.

2 When the cement is dry, place the plastic pot inside the ceramic container. Push the foam ball firmly onto the pole.

3 Choose lemons that are approximately all the same size to ensure a well shaped tree. To wire the lemons, first take a short stick and push it into the base of the lemon securely. As the lemons are heavy, for extra security take a ten-inch stub wire, push it straight through the base of the fruit, bring the ends down and twist around the top of the stick leaving a double leg.

5 Next add a circle of salal leaves either side of the lemon ring. The salal leaves are chosen because they resemble the lemons' own foliage. Some leaves should peep between the lemons to give a natural look of fruit with its foliage. Push the salal leaves firmly into the foam.

4 Start with a lemon in the top of the ball and push the stick and wires into the foam. The base of the fruit should rest on the foam. Make a circle of lemons around the foam ball to make the round shape.

6 Turn the tree ninety degrees and make another circle of lemons. These two circles with their even, round shape will act as a size and position guide when adding the other lemons.

7 Fill in the four sections between these two circles with lemons, adding leaves now and again between the fruit.

8 Finally, tuck leaves between the lemons to cover any foam, making sure the stems of the foliage go into the foam.

If the fruits are very heavy use wire netting over the foam ball to give additional security.

9 Once the top of the tree is complete, the base will require attention. Cover the cement and plastic pot with a layer of carpet moss.

For a smaller tree, try limes with bay (Laurus nobilis) foliage.

10 Finish with lemons placed on top of the moss. This will achieve continuity by bringing the color down to the base.

Choose a fruit to harmonize with the decor. Suggestions are: green apples interspersed with box (Buxus sp.) foliage; tangerines or small oranges with copper beech (Fagus sylvatica) foliage; shiny red apples with variegated holly (Ilex sp.), perfect for Christmas.

Bold and beautiful, this spectacular tree has a height of thirty inches, and will add zest to any party.

"The varied colours run: and while they break
On the charmed eye, the exulting florist marks,
With secret pride, the wonders of his hand…"

JAMES THOMSON (1700 - 1748), *SPRING FLOWERS*

CITRUS FRUITS AND FLOWERS IN THE ZINGY COLORS OF LIME, LEMON AND ORANGE COUPLED WITH THE BRILLIANT SKY BLUE POT
CREATE THIS CALIFORNIAN COCKTAIL FOR THE EYE.

mardi gras

FLOWERS

1. 20 stems Roses 'Orange Unique' (*Rosa* sp.)
2. 10 stems Statice (*Limonium sinuatum*)
3. 10 stems Celosia (*Celosia gargentea plumosa*)
4. 10 stems Hypericum 'Excellent flair' (*Hypericum* sp.)
5. 12 Galax leaves (*Galax viceolata*)

1

2

3

4

5

OTHER MATERIALS

Ceramic urn on a tripod, approx 14 inches high
Wet foam cone, 18 inches high
Carpet moss (*Minium* sp.)
/-inch stub wires
Paper ribbon in purple, lime and orange
3 dried seed balls
20 kumquats
Pink reel wire

All the vibrance and excitement of the Mardi Gras come together in this conical arrangement. The formal patterns of flowers, fruits and berries sweep around the symmetrical shape in bands of saturated color. This slender, cone-shaped design dates from Byzantine times when similar arrangements were made with jewel colors, ribbons and flowers. Placed on a wire pedestal, with its ethnic influences, it is a visual feast of riches.

Difficulty: Hard

METHOD

1 Soak the foam cone by holding it under running water until saturated. Push it into the container, the cone should fit snugly. Plug any gaps around the edges with pieces of wet foam to ensure the cone is firm and stable.

2 Make hairpins from the stub wires. Start by pinning moss onto the foam with the hairpins. This is wound around the cone to form the basic line for all the other materials to follow.

3 Make a frill of galax leaves around the base of the cone. Make sure the stems are pushed well into the foam. Twist the three paper ribbons together. Wire the ends of the ribbons together approximately 2 inches from the end, in a double-leg mount (see page 20). Push the wire into the base of the foam with the ribbon ends frilling out over the side of the container. Loop the ribbons up the cone, following the shape made by the moss. Hairpin into place at intervals. Finish at the top of the cone, securing the ends of the ribbons with another hairpin.

4 Cut the hypericum into short pieces and push them into the foam next to the ribbon, following the same winding shape. Keep all placements tightly grouped to create solid bands of color and texture. The roses follow the same pattern, butting up closely to the hypericum.

5 Continue adding bands of color and texture with a line of purple statice followed by celosia. As you work around the cone, make sure the slender shape remains, by packing the flowers tightly together in short groups.

6 Wire the kumquats by taking a seven inch length stub wire, and pushing it through the fruit so equal amounts of wire show either side. Bring the two wires together and twist close to the bottom of the fruit, making two legs of wire to push into the foam. Add the kumquats in close formation over the line of moss. Make another short group of roses at the base of the foam, where the kumquats finish, to cover any remaining exposed foam. The cone should now be completely covered with flowers, fruit and foliage.

It is the symmetry of the strong bands of vivid color and texture that give this design such strength and dominance. Coupled with the earthenware container, the tripod enhances and lightens this festival of flowing contours.

7 Using pink colored reel wire, attach the seed balls and three kumquats on short pieces of wire. Group them together at differing lengths, then firmly attach all the wires to a seven inch stub wire. Push this into the foam to one side of the cone and let the fruits and seed balls fall down over the edge of the container.

a compote of fruits

FLOWERS

1. 12 preserved red Roses (*Rosa* sp.)
2. 1 bunch green preserved Baby's Breath (*Gypsophila paniculata*)

1   2

OTHER MATERIALS

Flat piece of wood 10 x 3 inches
Dry floral foam
Red sinamay or similar open-weave ribbon
12-inch stub wires
Brown gutter percha
2 small clay pots
2 bundles of 24-inch twigs
10 dried chiles
6 dried orange slices
6 dried apple slices
Raffia
Red reindeer moss (*Cladonia rangifera*)
Glue gun

Preserved fruits and chiles make a wonderful decoration which is everlasting. In this design, orange and apple slices surround two old clay pots, with dried flowers, moss, and chiles grouped effectively to emphasize the rustic color scheme. Red sinamay ribbon links the whole design together and provides a light relief from the round-shaped fruits.

Difficulty: Hard

METHOD

1 Use a drill to make a small hole in the center top of the wooden board. Tape two stub wires together using gutter percha (see page 18) and push through the hole.

2 Twist the wires together just above the wooden board, make a round loop and twist the two wire ends into the loop to secure. Cut off any excess wire. Tape over the whole loop with gutter percha for extra security and a neat finish.

3 Cut up a block of dry floral foam to make two narrow strips to fit the wooden board. Glue in place with the glue gun.

4 Take the two bunches of twigs and tie together at one end with raffia, over the top of the foam-covered board.

6 Pass a stub wire through each clay pot, twist the wire ends together to form a double-leg mount. Cover the wire by tying raffia over and through the pot. Add the clay pots into the center of the foam. Use the glue gun to secure the underside of the pots to the foam.

Dried fruit slices can be purchased from your local florist, these will have been specially preserved. Drying your own orange slices is possible although the lasting qualities will not be as long as those commercially available.

8 Add the orange and apple slices by forming two groups of each, either side of the pots. Make two large groups of chiles at the top and base of the foam.

5 Pull the twig bundles together at the base of the foam and tie firmly with raffia. If necessary, also secure with a small amount of glue. The twigs should form a wigwam effect enclosing and covering the sides of the foam.

7 Wire the orange and apple slices plus the chiles in the same way: pass a stub wire through the fruit, then twist the wires together to form a double-leg mount.

It is possible to dry your own roses and baby's breath. Hang the flowers upside down in bunches in a warm place away from direct sunlight for about two to three weeks.

9 Take the dried baby's breath and add groups between the fruit slices to give an even outline. Bring some of the baby's breath into the center to carry the color through. Make hairpins with the stub wires. Attach the reindeer moss to the foam with these, again grouping it for maximum effect. Make sure all the wires are pushed firmly into the foam.

To dry an orange, cut it up into thin slices and arrange all the slices on a non-metallic plate so that they do not overlap. Cook on high in the microwave for approximately four minutes. Turn the slices over and cook again on high for another four minutes. The slices will still be moist so leave in a cool, airy place, turning the slices regularly. They will take up to two days to air-dry.

10 Starting at the top of the wall hanging, leave a small end of sinamay ribbon. Secure the ribbon in place with a hairpin, then loop and twist the ribbon over the design, securing into place several times with hairpins before finishing with a small tail of ribbon at the base of the design. Wedge a small piece of foam into the clay pots, then cut the red roses short and insert into the pots, pushing the stems into the foam. The roses should peep over the rim of the pots.

The finished wall hanging is ideal for a country kitchen wall, where its rustic charm and compote of fruits will give pleasure to the eye all year round.

seven

B R A N C H I N G   O U T

IN THE MASSED DESIGNS OF YESTERYEAR STEMS WERE THOUGHT

OF AS JUST A FUNCTIONAL PART OF A FLOWER AND EVERY

EFFORT WAS TAKEN TO HIDE THEM FROM VIEW. NOWADAYS OUR

APPROACH TO FLORAL ART IS LESS RIGID AND STUDYING THE

WAY THE FLOWER GROWS IN ITS NATURAL HABITAT HELPS US TO

DECIDE ON THE BEST WAY TO USE IT IN A DESIGN. RATHER THAN

BEING HIDDEN, STEMS CAN FORM AN INTEGRAL PART OF THE

DESIGN AS THIS CHAPTER ILLUSTRATES. TWIGS AND BRANCHES

HAVE ALWAYS HAD A ROLE IN FLOWER ARRANGING BUT AGAIN

THE WAY IN WHICH THEY ARE USED HAS EVOLVED

CONSIDERABLY OVER THE LAST FEW YEARS. THESE PROJECTS

EXPLORE THE VERSATILITY OF STEMS, TWIGS AND BRANCHES

AND SHOW HOW STUNNING EFFECTS CAN BE ACHIEVED.

a eucalyptus tree

1. 6 stems preserved Eucalyptus (*Eucalyptus* sp.)
2. Reindeer or Lichen moss (*Cladonia* sp.)

1   2

Sculptured trees are always popular and can be made in a variety of leaves. The eucalyptus used on this tree has been preserved so it will last for a very long time. An interesting feature is the use of pins to secure the leaves to the foam ball, as they become part of the decoration. With the texture of studded leather and the appearance of a geometric sculpture, the finished tree will make a dramatic feature in your home and inevitably become a talking point.

Difficulty: Intermediate

METHOD

OTHER MATERIALS

Ceramic container approx 6 inches diameter
9-inch twig
½-inch silver knob pins
Dry foam sphere, 4 inches diameter
Dry foam block
Glue gun
Hairpins

1 Cut the dry foam block to size and fit snugly into the container. The foam should be level with the top of the container. Use a glue gun to glue the sides of the foam to the container. Choose a twig strong enough to hold the sphere of foam, with an interesting curve or shape. Firmly push the twig into the foam, then secure the twig to the foam with glue.

2 Take the leaves carefully off the stem of the eucalyptus. Leave the leaves at the top of the stem as they will be too small to use.

When making a large sculpture, ensure the stick used is firmly anchored into the base. For floor standing sculptures it is a good idea to cement the stick in place.

3 Push the dry foam sphere onto the top of the twig and secure in place with glue. Once the glue is dry, start to attach the leaves to the ball. Take five eucalyptus leaves, position in the center at the top of the ball. Overlap the leaves in the center to make a flower pattern. Push a knob pin through the center of the "flower" to secure all the leaves. Push the pin firmly through the leaves and into the foam until only the knob is visible.

These kinds of sculptures can be made in many materials, either preserved or, for a special occasion, fresh flowers. Ideal leaves to use are box (Buxus sp.) copper beach, (Fagus sylvatica), oak (Quercus sp.), and ivy (Hedera sp.).

4 Work around the sphere in a circle, overlapping each leaf in a neat pattern so that no foam shows between the leaves. Secure each leaf near the top center edge with a pin.

Pre-formed foam shapes can easily be purchased, in both dry and wet foam. Cones and spheres are the most popular shapes.

The secret of creating wonderful sculptures is to keep the shape neat and uncluttered. The eucalyptus stems in this design relieve the round form and give movement to the finished tree which is dynamic and impressive to view.

5 Once the ball is completed, remove any remaining leaves from two of the eucalyptus stems. Push them firmly into the foam, then bring them over the top of the sphere and secure to the top with a wire hairpin. Use the reindeer moss to finish the base, by hairpinning over the foam in an even covering.

Try making your own shape by sculpting a block of dry foam into animal shapes. Use wire netting around the foam to support it if necessary.

Care must be taken when using electrical appliances. Keep away from water and disconnect when not in use.

entwined

FLOWERS

1. 7 Calla Lilies (*Zantedeschia* sp.)
2. 3 Allium 'Purple Sensation' (*Allium* sp.)
3. 10 Carnations (*Dianthus* sp.)
4. 7 stems Statice (*Limonium sinautum*)

1   2

3   4

OTHER MATERIALS

Open wire basket 10 x 6½ inches
Plastic tray to fit inside the basket
Floral foam
Floral tape
Carpet moss
2 14-inch twig bundles
Tying material
Hair pins

This is an unusual modern style of arrangement which uses new design techniques to produce seemingly perpetual motion, with the callas entwined in twigs, twisting in different directions. The use of solid groups of intense color on the base of the arrangement add depth and dimension to this energetic design.

Difficulty: Hard

METHOD

1 Place a block of wet foam onto the plastic tray and secure firmly to the tray with floral tape. Using wire hairpins attach groups of moss to the sides of the foam, leaving spaces for some flowers. Tie one of the twig bundles to the front of the basket.

2 Fit the tray into the basket, then add a pathway of moss across the top of the foam, securing in place with hairpins.

Many flowers and twigs will allow their stems to be manipulated to go in the direction you wish. Fleshy stems will curve most easily.

4 Use the remaining twigs to form a twisting cage above the flowers. Loop and coil the twigs then push the ends into the foam securely, so that the whole basket is entwined with twigs.

3 Add groups of carnations to the sides and top of the foam to create bold blocks of color. The carnations should sit close to each other, with the heads almost resting on the foam. Add the statice in a similar way to create more strong areas of color. Undo one of the twig bundles and tie roughly half to the back of the basket.

Keep stroking the stems gently to make them curve, or wind them around the inside of a bucket to encourage them to curl.

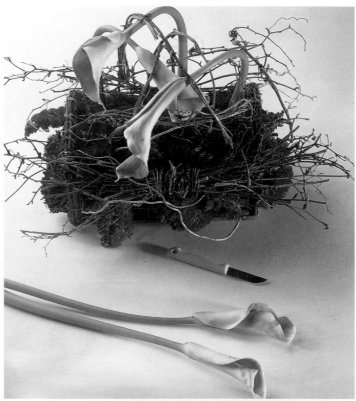

5 The stems of the lilies will bend and curve if manipulated carefully and gently. By stroking the stem in the direction you wish it to go, it will start to curve. Cut the first calla stems and push into the foam at the back of the arrangement. Carefully loop the stems through the twigs which will hold the flower in place.

6 Try to make as many looping stems as possible to create movement. The calla heads should all face in different directions as the backs of the flowers are as important as the fronts.

If twigs such as willow are brittle, soak them in water to make them supple.

The twisting stems embrace and frame the whole design, creating the feeling of energetic activity, with the eye coming to rest on the solid forms of the carnations at the base.

"*I* *have a garden of my own*
But so with roses overgrown,
And lilies, that you would it guess,
To be a little wilderness."

ANDREW MARVELL (1621 - 1678),
THE NYMPH COMPLAINING FOR THE DEATH OF HER FAWN

enclosure

In this design emphasis is placed on the beauty of the lilies by enclosing them in a cage of twigs. The straight, parallel stems of the wood attract the eye to the rounder form of the lilies, accentuating their beauty. These twigs also act as a supporting structure for the lily stems and result in a dramatic effect which uses just a few of these elegant flowers.

Difficulty: Easy

FLOWERS

1. 6 stems Lilies 'Johan Vermeer' (*Lilium* sp.)
2. 3 stems pink Statice (*Limonium sinuatum*)
3. Rosemary (*Rosmarinus officinalis*)
4. Galax leaves (*Galax viceolata*)
5. Box (*Buxus* sp.)

OTHER MATERIALS

Pink bowl, 9 inch diameter, 5 inch depth
30 pink Ting tings
Floral foam
Raffia
7-inch stub wires

METHOD

1 Fill the container with wet foam. Trim twenty four ting tings to approximately twenty inches high. Make four groups of six. Keep any trimmed stems to use for the horizontal bars. Push the groups of ting tings into the foam to form a square around the outer edges of the container.

2 Make two horizontal bars to go across the top of the twigs. Position one across the two back groups and the other across the two front groups of ting tings. Tie in place neatly and securely with raffia.

A structure can be made from any twigs. Birch (Betula sp.) and willow (Salix sp.) are good choices, the latter is particularly pliable and will bend to form arches or circular shapes. Even thick stems which might be discarded can be used for support. Experiment by making horizontal or circular structures for a different effect.

3 Soften the edge of the container with placements of galax leaves, rosemary, box and statice. Place in groups around the container, making sure all the stems are pushed well into the foam.

4 Add three tall lily stems into the center of the cage, cutting the stem ends diagonally and pushing well into the foam. The flower heads should be just below the top of the ting tings. Add another slightly shorter lily stem to the front of the design.

5 Make two more horizontal bars as described in step two. Position the bars underneath the shortest lily. Fill in the base of the arrangement using open lily heads, almost touching the foam. Intersperse statice and foliage with the lilies until the whole of the foam is covered.

6 Wire a group of ting tings together on a double-leg mount. Tie with raffia in the center and insert into the front of the arrangement to add whisps of twig at the base. This arrangement will be extremely long lasting. Water daily by taking to a sink and carefully pouring water over the foam, then allowing to drain. Always put a mat under arrangements to protect the table.

Making a cage or enclosure for flowers is a clever way of supporting stems too weak to stand on their own. This is often the case with lilies whose heads are so heavy the stems often break under the weight.

A stylish arrangement in a luminous pink color harmony that shows the striking elegance of the flowers in a contemporary design.

passing strangers

FLOWERS

1. 6 Birds of Paradise (*Strelitzia reginae*)
2. 5 Carnations 'Solar' (*Dianthus* sp.)
3. 4 stems Spray Chrysanthemums 'Santini Kermit' (*Chrysanthemum* sp.)
4. 4 Ming fern (*Asparagus myriocladus*)
5. 15 Galax leaves (*Galax viceolata*)
6. 15 Ivy leaves (*Hedera helix*)

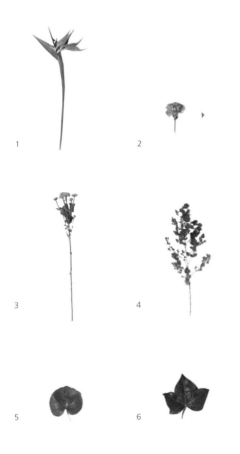

1   2

3   4

5   6

OTHER MATERIALS

10-inch foam posy pad and plastic base
7-inch stub wires (optional)

Aristocrats among flowers, the majestic Birds of Paradise certainly match their namesakes with their flamboyant display. Here is a classic case where the beauty of the stem should not be hidden but fully utilized in the design. The stems are emphasized in *Passing Strangers* by using the flowers diagonally, drawing the eye to the beauty of both flower and stem. The subtle, textured base acts as a perfect foil to the dominant, theatrical flowers.

Difficulty: Intermediate

METHOD

1   Cut away the edges of the posy pad to give a rounded look. Take the posy pad to a sink and immerse in water for a few minutes. Drain off any excess water.

2   Some of the ivy leaves may need to be wired for support. Make a neat stitch three quarters of the way up the main vein. Pull the wire through the leaf, till the wire is of equal length each side of the stitch. Draw the wires down to the top of the stem to form a loop. Wrap one end of the wire firmly around the top of the stem and the other wire. The wire will form double legs. Do not cut the stem off, as this must penetrate the foam to allow the leaf to drink.

3 Group the ivy and the galax leaves around the edge of the foam leaving spaces for the ming fern. Angle the leaves downward so they just touch the table top. Make sure all the stems are in the foam.

5 The second bird of paradise is the same height as the first, placed diagonally in the opposite direction, with the stems crossing. Add the remaining bird of paradise flowers gradually reducing the length of stem, to form the criss-cross pattern. The last flowers are placed low onto the base.

4 Fill in neatly with ming fern around the edges of the foam, between the ivy and galax leaves. The edge of the base should now be covered with foliage. Take the tallest bird of paradise flower and place it at an angle with the stem going into the foam just off-center. This flower is roughly twice the length of the container.

This is an ideal way to display such flamboyant flowers. Full of self-importance, these kings among flowers have the right to vanity.

6 Finish off the base by using flowers and foliage in irregular groups of differing textures. Group ming fern and ivy across the base to make pathways, and make several groups of spray chrysanthemums with the heads all at the same low level on the foam. Finally, finish off with two groups of orange carnations, again with the stems cut short so that the heads almost rest on the foam. The foam should be completely covered with flowers and foliage. Water daily by taking the arrangement to a sink and pouring water over the base, allow to drain.

"The laughing leaves of the trees divide,
And screen from seeing and leave in sight..."

A.C. **SWINBURNE** (1837 - 1909), *ATALANTA IN CALYDON*

GROUPED TOGETHER, THESE EUCALYPTUS TREES CREATE A STRIKING SCULPTURAL DISPLAY. AS THE TREES ARE SO LONG LASTING,
THE POTS CAN BE REARRANGED FROM TIME TO TIME TO VARY THE EFFECT.

eight

THE SEASHORE

SEA, SAND AND SHELLS AWAKEN CHILDHOOD MEMORIES OF LONG SUMMER DAYS AT THE BEACH, DELVING INTO ROCK-POOLS, FISHING FOR CRABS, AND FINDING SHELL TREASURES TO TAKE HOME. BRINGING THE SEASIDE INTO OUR HOMES CAN BE EASILY ACHIEVED. THE BLEACHED NATURAL COLORS OF THE SEASHORE ARE SOFT AND EASY TO LIVE WITH, MAKING CALM, RELAXING DESIGNS. MARITIME DESIGNS ARE PARTICULARLY APPEALING USED IN BATHROOMS.

THERE ARE SO MANY SHELLS AVAILABLE NOW THAT DECIDING WHAT TO CHOOSE CAN BE CONFUSING. START BY PLAYING WITH A GROUP OF DIFFERENT SHAPED AND TEXTURED SHELLS AND PEBBLES, LIE THEM ON A BED OF SILVER SAND IN A SHALLOW GLASS BOWL AND SEE HOW GOOD THEY LOOK TOGETHER.

beachcomber

Exotic shells, washed up on distant shores, are grouped casually around the edge of a shallow basket to make a special holder for fragrant potpourri. The shells are entwined with old rope, and finished with bundles of twigs and starfish to bring the atmosphere of the seaside into your home. The display will, of course, last and last. Revive the potpourri from time to time with a few drops of essential oils.

Difficulty: Easy

METHOD

MATERIALS

Shallow basket with handles, approx 10 inches diameter
30 shells of differing shapes, sizes and colors
3 starfish
Rope
Raffia
2 bundles of twigs
Potpourri
Glue gun

1 Make two rope bows, tie them securely in the center with raffia.

2 Attach the rope bows to the basket handle by tying with raffia.

6 Entwine the rope between the shell placements, looping it to give movement to the design. Glue into place several times around the edge of the basket. Finally add potpourri to the basket to finish the design.

3 Take six shells of different shapes, sizes and colors which will complement each other. Glue them securely together with the glue gun to make interesting patterns. Make six groups of shells like this.

5 Continue to add the groups of shells until the edge of the basket is covered. Take two bundles of twigs and the starfish, add to either side of the basket edge, gluing in place.

The finished basket will scent your home for many weeks. Once the fragrance has evaporated it can be revived with a few drops of essential oils.

4 When the glue is dry, attach the shell groups to the edge of the basket. Add glue to the underside of the shells and stick firmly to the rim of the basket. Hold the shells in place until the glue is dry. Neat gluing is essential, only a small amount is necessary, as the glue should not be seen once the basket is finished.

mermaids

FLOWERS

1. 2 stems Sea Holly (*Eringium orion*)
2. 10 stems Brodiacea (*Triteleia* sp.)

Inspired by the colors and myths of the sea, this light-hearted design combines elements of land and sea. The mother-of-pearl shells glint and glimmer in the light like silvery mermaids, shimmering in a mirage. The simple twig structure supports the shells above the ripples of blue sea holly and brodiacea to create a simple, informal design.

Difficulty: Intermediate

METHOD

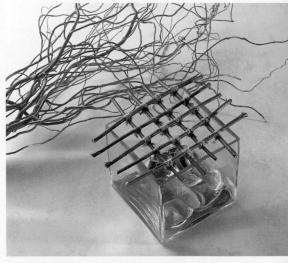

OTHER MATERIALS

Glass tank 6 inches square
10 sticks 8½ inches long
30 shells
Raffia
String
Twisted Willow (*Salix tortuosa*)

1 Make a simple trellis to fit over the top of the tank. Lay out five of the sticks then place the other five sticks on top to form a grid. Make sure this is the correct size to sit on top of the glass tank. Tie the sticks together where they meet with string.

2 Place some of the shells in the base of the tank, keeping twelve to hang on the branches. Sit the trellis on top of the tank.

3 Fill the container with water. Trim the twigs so that they are approximately thirty inches tall. Add the twigs to the container in an informal style, threading the branches through the trellis into the container.

4 Add the sea holly in between the twigs, with the trellis supporting the stems and keeping them in position. Cut the stems to differing heights to form an interesting pattern.

6 Take twelve shells and tie raffia firmly through the top hole in each one.

7 Tie the shells to the branches at differing heights so they dangle between the twigs.

5 The brodiacea should be used to give height to the arrangement and to break up the solid form of the sea holly. Cut the stems diagonally and place through the design.

As though blown by sea-winds, the shell mermaids dance in the light, with the sea holly forming a tide of blue waves beneath them.

"...Every flower,
The pink, the jessamine, the wall-flower, the carnation,
The jonquil, the mild lily, opes her heavens; every tree
And flower and herb soon fill the air with an innumerable dance,
Yet all in order sweet and lovely..."

WILLIAM BLAKE (1757 - 1827), *THE VISION OF BEULAH*

PRETTY COLUMBINE, ARRANGED LOOSELY IN A GLASS JUG, MAKE A QUICK AND EASY DISPLAY.

neptune's treasure

Wall hanging designs are a brilliant idea for small rooms where space is at a premium, but some form of decoration is necessary. This twig ring decorated with shells, rope and raffia is ideal for hanging in a bathroom or small cloakroom. It is quick to make and easy to achieve an exciting nautical look.

Difficulty: Easy

METHOD

MATERIALS

12-inch twig ring
2 12-inch stub wires
Brown gutter percha tape
25 shells of differing shapes, sizes and colors
Rope
Raffia
2 Starfish
Glue gun

1 Make a strong hanging loop by taping together two stub wires with gutter percha tape (see page 18). Thread the taped wire through the twig ring, twist the wire together close to the ring. Form a small loop, then trim off any excess wire and twist the ends together into the loop. When secure, cover with gutter percha tape to conceal the wire ends and give a neat finish.

2 Choose five shells of differing shapes, texture and color and group them to form an interesting pattern. Glue the shells together using the glue gun. Make three groups.

3 Glue the three shell groups onto the twig ring, with equal distance between each group. Use a small amount of glue on the underside of the shells, firmly stick to the ring and hold in place until the glue is dry.

4 Add one or two smaller shells between the shell groups. Glue the starfish either side of the ring. Then entwine with the rope, forming interesting loops, and securing at intervals around the ring with glue. Finally make two raffia bows and glue into place either side of the ring. Wait until all the glue is dry, and everything is securely fastened to the ring before hanging.

Once finished the shell ring will make an affordable alternative to an expensive picture, making a wall come alive with this personal, eye-catching decoration.

the candlelit shore

FLOWERS

1. 2 stems Lilies 'San Jose' (*Lilium* sp.)
2. 2 stems Kangaroo Paw (*Anigoxanthos* sp.)
3. 6 Roses 'Prohyta' (*Rosa* sp.)
4. 2 stems Kochia (*Maireana sedifolia*)
5. 4 stems *Senecio greyii*
6. Ivy (*Hedera helix*)

1   2

3   4

5   6

OTHER MATERIALS

Glass plate, 14 inches diameter
Glass candle holder, 14 inches high
10-inch church candle
Floral foam
3 scented candles in 3- inch terracotta pots
2 small terracotta dishes approx 3 inches diameter
Silver sand
Shells
2 starfish

Waves lapping on a moonlit shore provide the perfect setting for a romantic dinner and this arrangement captures that vision and brings it into the dining-room. Scented candles add to the sentimental imagery. One of the advantages of this arrangement is that it can be left permanently on display, as it still looks stylish without the flower arrangements.

Difficulty: Easy

METHOD

1 Pour enough silver sand into the candle holder to hold the candle upright. Add a few small shells to the top of the sand for decoration.

2 Place the candle holder in the center of the glass plate. Sprinkle sand onto the plate. Choose shells for their interesting shape, color and texture, make two groups either side of the candle holder. Fill the two terracotta pots with wet foam, place between the shell groups, together with the two candles in terracotta pots.

3 Make two small, identical arrangements in the terracotta pots. Begin by covering the rim of the pots with ivy leaves.

4 Add an open lily to the center of each arrangement, cutting the stem end diagonally and pushing firmly into the foam. The roses are grouped in two placements either side of the lily.

5 Finish the arrangement by adding kochia and kangaroo paw to give depth of color to the design. Fill in where necessary with ivy to cover the foam. Just before dinner, light the candles.

The soft peachy tones of the flowers enhance the natural colors of the shells, with the candlelight providing a warm glow for a perfect evening setting.

Candles can be a fire hazard.
Do not leave a lit candle unattended.
Keep all materials well away from the naked flame.

nine

WONDERFUL WEAVES

TEXTILES HAVE ALWAYS HAD A ROLE TO PLAY WITHIN FLOWER
ARRANGEMENT. RIBBONS ARE USED LAVISHLY, PARTICULARLY IN
WEDDING DESIGNS. FABRICS REFLECT DIFFERING FLAVORS IN
STYLE: RICH SILKS, DAMASKS AND VELVETS WILL ADD GLAMOR
TO ARRANGEMENTS; FINE SHEERS SUCH AS CHEESECLOTH,
ORGANDIE AND MUSLIN CREATE A PRETTY SUMMER WEDDING
LOOK; IN CONTRAST HESSIANS, ROPES AND BLEACHED LINENS
CREATE A HOMESPUN, NATURAL EFFECT.

CHOOSE THE LOOK YOU WISH TO EMULATE AND TRY NOT TO
MIX TOO MANY TEXTURES TOGETHER AS IT CAN BECOME
CONFUSING TO THE EYE. WHICHEVER STYLE OF DESIGN YOU ARE
MAKING, THE USE OF FABRICS MUST BE WELL THOUGHT OUT,
AND INTRODUCED AS AN INTEGRAL PART OF THE DESIGN, NOT
SOMETHING THAT IS ADDED LATER JUST TO FILL UP A SPACE.

indian summer

Ethnic in origin, this simple yet distinctive mobile is ideal for hanging over a buffet table at teenagers' parties where fun styles and vibrant colors will catch the imagination of young people.

Difficulty: Easy

FLOWERS

1. 2 orange Gerbera 'Venturi' (*Gerbera* sp.)
2. 4 strands Bear grass (*Xerophyllum tenax*)

OTHER MATERIALS

4 canes measuring 20 inches, 15 inches, 13 inches, 10 inches
2 glass phials
4 colored, skeletonized, magnolia leaves
Pink reel wire
String
Yarns and threads of your choice
16 brightly colored beads
3 brightly colored feathers

METHOD

1 Start by wrapping the glass phials with a skeletonized leaf, tie in place with thread or yarn. Tie string around the top of the phial and make a hanging loop.

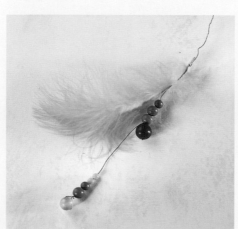

2 Take a length of pink reel wire, thread four of the beads onto the wire, twisting the wire around the first bead to secure. Leave a two inch gap, then add another four beads. Finally add a feather above the beads, twisting the wire around the end of the feather to secure.

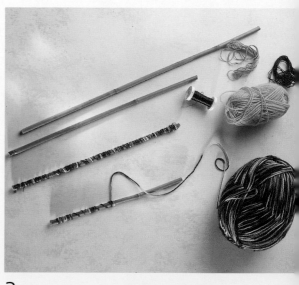

3 Decorate the canes by twisting brightly colored wool, embroidery threads, ribbons and colored wires around the sticks until they have a rainbow effect. Twist a piece of wire around the ends of each stick to keep the yarns in place.

4 Tie the four canes together at different angles to make an interesting shape. Secure together with pink reel wire. Add a string hanger to the top cane.

6 Add the feather trails, one to the top horizontal cane the other on the opposite side of the mobile at the lower join. Secure with wire. Add two skeletonized magnolia leaves to the remaining joins.

7 Twist yarn around two strands of bear grass, put the ends of the grass into one phial, tie the tip of the grass to the top bar. Do the same with the other phial but bring the grass down to tie on the bottom cane. Add water to the phials and place a gerbera in each phial.

5 Attach the two phials to the top bar with pink reel wire. Make one longer than the other to give a more pleasing look.

Mobiles are fun and easy to make. Try experimenting by placing the canes in different positions to create unusual shapes.

dreamer

A dreamy summer haze of miniature roses, lilies and cow parsley arranged loosely in a country style makes a charming display for any occasion. To give new life to an old container, it has been wrapped in cheesecloth and finished with a lace bow. The fabric and trimming complete the soft, ethereal look of this simple design.

Difficulty: Intermediate

FLOWERS

1. 8 stems Cow Parsley 'Ami Majus' (*Anthriscus sylvestris*)
2. 8 stems spray Roses 'Evelyn' (*Rosa* sp.)
3. 5 stems Lilies 'Monte Rosa' (*Lilium* sp.)
4. 20 stems Bear grass (*Xerophyllum tenax*)

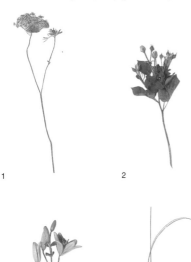

1

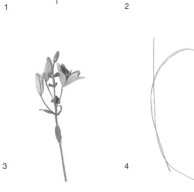

3   4

OTHER MATERIALS

Old container 10 inches high
Piece of cheesecloth to cover pot
Peach ribbons, ½ inch wide
Lace ribbon, 2 inches wide

METHOD

1 Lay out the cheesecloth on a table, place the container in the center, then gather up the material evenly just under the rim of the container. Tie the muslin in place with a length of narrow peach ribbon. Tidy the top of the muslin so that it forms a frill above the tying point.

At Christmas, use wrapping papers and glitter thread with a group of shiny baubles hanging from the bow.

2 Make a figure-of-eight bow with the lace (see page 23), leaving two long trails to hang down the front of the vase. Tie in place, then add a bow of pale peach ribbon over the lace. Fill the container with water.

3 Use the cow parsley as a filler to hold the stems of roses and lilies in place. Arrange in a loose, free style, cutting some stems shorter at the front and sides.

Try using brown paper and tying with raffia for a rustic look.

5 Position the lilies, recessed slightly, with the open ones toward the center of the arrangement. Finally add wisps of bear grass to give movement and delicacy to the design.

Materials like cheesecloth, which are soft and drape well, are easiest to use. If the cheesecloth is too white, soak it for half an hour in cold tea, then wash it again and it will become a lovely creamy color.

4 Add the spray roses next, pushing the stems into the container between the cow parsley, which should hold the stems in place. Again arrange in a loose style.

An old container is given a new lease of life in this romantic, hazy summer style of arrangement in soft, dreamy colors.

"*A* *lovely being, scarcely formed or moulded,*
A rose with all its sweetest leaves yet folded."

LORD BYRON (1788 - 1824), *DON JUAN*

grand gala

For sheer luxury the opulence of large red roses fashioned into a chair back, finished with a luxurious net and satin ribbon bow, together with a burgundy tassel, makes a dramatic statement for a grand occasion.

Difficulty: Hard

FLOWERS

1. 8 red Roses 'Grand Gala' (*Rosa* sp.)
2. 1 Spray Rose 'Tomango' (*Rosa* sp.)
3. 6 long trails of Ivy (*Hedera helix*)
4. 5 stems *Alchemilla mollis*

1

2

3

4

OTHER MATERIALS

Florist's adhesive tape
Tying twine
Red net, 1½ yards
Stiffened gold edged red ribbon
Red ribbon, ¼ inch wide
Curtain tassel

METHOD

1 Make a figure-of-eight bow with the red net, leaving two long trails of net.

2 Take a length of narrow red ribbon and tie firmly in the center of the bow to hold the bow shape in position. Leave two long ends of ribbon for tying around the back of the chair.

3 Remove any leaves and clean all the stems which will be below the tying point. Lie the flowers out in groups on a table.

4 Start with a small bunch of alchemilla in the hand, then add four of the single red roses, the tallest in the center, add more alchemilla to the sides and front. This is a small posy: from the tying point to the top of the tallest flower should be no more than five inches, otherwise it will restrict the movement of the chair's occupant.

6 When the top of the posy is finished add long trails of ivy to the front and side for a luxuriant effect. Use twine to wrap around the binding point and tie firmly with a double knot (see pages 23–24). Trim off any excessively long stems.

Tied designs for chairbacks should be added at the last moment to ensure they last throughout the party.

5 Continue to add the remaining single roses and spray rose, filling in between with alchemilla. Remember this design should have a flat back so that it will sit well on the back of the chair.

7 Using florist's adhesive tape, attach the posy to the back of the chair, firmly wrapping the tape around the chair and the tying point of the posy several times, until the posy is firmly attached to the chair. Make sure this is neat. If it is an expensive chair where adhesive tape could cause damage, use ribbon or twine to tie in place.

If your budget is
small, just add a
raffia bow and trails
of ivy.

8 Lift the ivy trails and slip the net bow
underneath. Take the two long ribbon ties on the
net bow over the back of the chair in opposite
directions to cover the adhesive tape, then bring
them back around the chair to tie under the
flowers at the tying point. Make a bow with
luxurious satin ribbon using the figure-of-eight
method shown on page 23. Tie it into the center
of the net bow using the long ribbon ties to
secure it in place. Finally add the tassel, again
tying into the center of the bow with the long
ribbon ties.

*If the chairbacks are
to last all day, make
the decorations in
floral foam so that the
flowers will last
longer. Special foam
holders with clips to
attach to the back of
the chair can be
obtained from florists.*

*Add these decorations to every chair to create
theatrical grandeur for that special gala occasion.*

texture

FLOWERS

1. 4 *Agapanthus*
2. 5 stems Button Chrysanthemums 'Statesman' (*Chrysanthemum* sp.)
3. 3 stems spray Chrysanthemums 'Reagan Yellow' (*Chrysanthemum* sp.)
4. 2 bunches blue Cornflowers (*Centaurea cyanus*)
5. Ivy leaves (*Hedera helix*)
6. Cypress (*Cupressus* sp.)
7. Typha leaves (*Liriope muscari*)

OTHER MATERIALS

Shallow, oblong tray, 14 x 10 inches
Floral foam
Colored string
Paper twist ribbon
Blue picot edged ribbon, ½ inch wide
5 string-covered balls
Carpet moss (*Minum* sp.)
Hairpins
Glue gun

Textural interest is important in giving another dimension to the visual effect of any finished arrangement. Here, differing textures and shapes are used in groups and bands of strong color, with the grass wrapped with ribbon and string to form contrasting elements within the design.

Difficulty: Intermediate

METHOD

1 Soak the floral foam. Fill the container with the foam, rounding off the edges slightly.

2 Start by making up groups of foliage around the edges, and into the center with cypress and ivy. Also make pathways of moss across the top of the foam, pinning in place.

Paper ribbon, yarns and fabric are great for adding texture to an arrangement.

4 Make large groups of cornflowers and button chrysanthemums in between the foliage groups. Cut the flower stems at an angle and push the stems firmly into the foam.

3 Take the paper twist ribbon, open out then make loops across the foam from one side of the arrangement to the other. Hairpin in place between the loops. Position the string-covered balls to form groups either side of the ribbon.

An arrangement of all one color, particularly all white or foliage designs, will need more textural interest to avoid looking monotonous.

5 Use the yellow chrysanthemums and the agapanthus to finish the groups of flowers. The foam should now be completely covered with flowers and foliage.

Textures can dramatically change the effect of an arrangement, it can also suggest different moods and emotions.

6 Add a small amount of glue to the tip of a typha leaf, wind the ribbon down the leaf to the base and glue the end with the glue gun. Make six in total with string and ribbon.

7 Push the stem of the typha leaf into the foam, loop the grass over the arrangement and hairpin the top of the leaf into place approximately two inches from the tip. Continue to add the typha leaves looping and forming patterns over the strong textured base.

This type of design is ideal for using flowers with broken or weak stems, and because of the shortness of the stem the arrangement will last for many weeks if kept watered.

ten

INDOOR GARDENS

CREATING A GARDEN IN A BOWL CAN BE AN EASY WAY OF BRINGING NATURE INTO YOUR HOME. IT MAKES AN IDEAL PRESENT FOR THE CITY DWELLER, AND THE JOY OF SEEING A PLANT YOU HAVE LOVINGLY CARED FOR GROW AND THRIVE GIVES ENORMOUS PLEASURE. IF YOU WANT YOUR PLANTS TO PROSPER THEY WILL NEED ADEQUATE LIGHT, HEAT, AND WATER. NOT ALL PLANTS LIKE THE SAME ENVIRONMENT, SO TAKE CARE TO CHECK IF YOU ARE PLANTING DIFFERENT VARIETIES TOGETHER THAT THEY ALL LIKE THE SAME CONDITIONS.

PLANTS WILL LOOK MUCH MORE INTERESTING IF THEY ARE GROUPED TOGETHER RATHER THAN DOTTED AROUND IN SEPARATE POTS. TRY CAPTURING A NATURAL SCENE WITHIN A BOWL; A WOODLAND WALK, A FOREST GLADE, OR MAKE A DESIGN STATEMENT USING ARCHITECTURAL PLANTS WITH STRONG AND DISTINCTIVE FORMS. THIS CHAPTER GIVES YOU A RANGE OF IDEAS TO TRY, WHY NOT THEN COME UP WITH SOME ARRANGEMENTS OF YOUR OWN.

marguerites

1. 7 Marguerite plants (*Chrysanthemum frutescens*)

1

A summery profusion of marguerites is a perfect planted design for outdoor living. Although they will live indoors on a sunny windowsill, marguerites are most suited to living outside, where these pretty daisies will keep on flowering all summer long. This makes them a sound investment for a deck or terrace table. Keep them in a sunny spot and water daily for maximum effect.

Difficulty: Easy

METHOD

1 Using the glue gun, glue a band of lime green paper ribbon around each bucket, approximately one and a half inches from the top rim. Hold in place until the glue is dry.

2 Line the basket with damp moss. Attach three of the buckets along the handle of the basket with raffia.

OTHER MATERIALS

1 large basket, 11 x 11 inches lined with plastic
4 small white buckets, 4 inches diameter
Lime green paper ribbon
Raffia
Carpet moss (*Minum* sp.)
Glue gun

Keep removing flowers which have died to encourage new flowers to grow through.

3 Keep the marguerites in their pots and arrange four in the basket. Leave a space at the side of the basket in the front for a white bucket to be added.

5 Add the remaining marguerites to the buckets tied on the handles.

4 Place a white bucket in the space at the side of the basket, wedging it in between the plants. Fill in any gaps between the plants with moss, covering the pots neatly. The moss will also help to keep the plants moist. The plants can be taken out individually to water, or alternatively you could plant them all into soil if preferred.

The dewy freshness of the green and white color harmony is cooling to the eye on a balmy summer's evening. Perfect for an al fresco party.

butterflies

With grace and elegance these beautiful white orchids reign supreme over a green bamboo container. The flower heads flutter between contorted willow, adding movement and rhythm to the design. A green and white color scheme is always tranquil, and part of this arrangement's beauty is the space within the design which adds to the dignity of the orchids.

Difficulty: Easy

FLOWERS

1. 3 white Moth Orchid plants (*Phalaenopsis* sp.)
2. 1 *Helxine soleirolii*
3. Moss

1

2

3

OTHER MATERIALS

Bamboo or basket container, deep enough to
    hold the plant pots
Strong polythene sheeting
Contorted willow (*Salix tortuosa*)
Pebbles
Raffia

METHOD

1 Line the container with plastic sheeting and add a layer of damp moss to the base.

2 Add the orchid plants in their pots, arranging the tallest to the back with the heads dancing in different directions.

Orchids can live happily indoors and if given the right conditions will bloom for many months. Keep the plant in a small pot, with a bark compost for easy drainage. Place in a warm but shady spot, away from direct sunlight and feed regularly.

3 Place the helxine at the front of the container to creep over the edge, again leaving it in its pot.

Phalaenopsis orchids will not tolerate low temperatures. A moist atmosphere is essential, so spray the plant regularly with water and keep the soil moist at all times.

4 Insert the contorted willow by pushing it into the soil in the pots, then twist it around the orchids, and tie to the orchid stems with raffia.

5 Surround and cover the pots with damp moss. Finish with groups of pebbles to form an interesting, textured base.

The aerial roots which spring over the sides of the pot are part of the beauty of the plant.

This planted arrangement is designed so that the plants are left in their own pots and can be easily removed from the container if necessary. Keep in a well-lit spot but away from direct sunlight.

"*Love guards the roses of thy lips*
And flies about them like a bee;
If I approach he forward skips,
And if I kiss he stingeth me."

THOMAS LODGE (1558 - 1625), *LOVE GUARDS THE ROSES OF THY LIPS*

a spring garden

FLOWERS

1. 2 Hyacinth 'City of Haarlem' (*Hyacinthus* sp.)
2. 4 Miniature Narcissi 'Tête à Tête' (*Narcissi* sp.)
3. 2 Variegated Ivy (*Hedera helix*)
4. 4 Primroses (*Primula acaulis*)
5. 1 Grape Hyacinth (*Muscari* sp.)

The delights of a spring garden are captured in this rustic basket filled with old clay pots and spring plants. Miniature daffodils are ideal for planting indoors, and once they have finished flowering, can be planted outside to flower again next year. The hyacinths bring a welcome perfume to the arrangement, with the primulas adding color to the design. This type of planted arrangement does not have to be confined indoors, it can be left outdoors on a garden table, or in a conservatory. Alternatively, place it on a terrace where it can be seen from indoors and outside, or in a porch to welcome guests.

Difficulty: Intermediate

METHOD

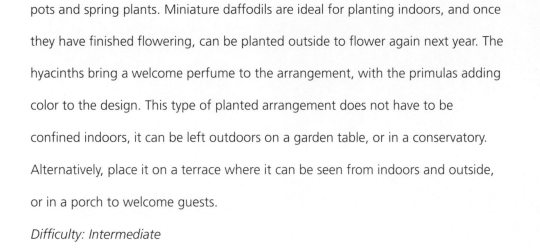

OTHER MATERIALS

Trug basket, 16 x 12 inches, lined with plastic sheeting
Selection of old clay pots, some broken
Potting compost
Raffia
Bundle of twigs
Moss
Stub wires

1 Add a layer of soil to the base of the basket. Arrange groups of old pots with spaces between them, broken pots can also look interesting.

2 Remove the ivies from their pots and plant to trail over the rim of the basket at the front.

4 Thread raffia through a small clay pot. Plant one small narcissus into it, and tie to the top of the handle to give the arrangement additional height. Then tie two small empty old clay pots to the front of the handle. Finish off by decorating with bundles of twigs attached with double leg mounts covered over with raffia.

Read the care instructions on the plant when purchasing and only water and feed when necessary.

3 Plant one pot of miniature narcissi into the center of the basket, and the others into the clay pots at the back. Add the grape hyacinth and hyacinths to the arrangement, then place the primroses with the brightest colors toward the center of the basket. Firm all the plants in with soil, then cover with moss to give a neat finish.

Choose plants which will suit your environment. Do not choose a plant which likes cool conditions and then place it in a hot dry office – it's asking for trouble. Seek advice from the florist before purchasing.

The simple, country style of this rustic basket will bring the freshness of a spring morning into your home. To ensure your arrangement lasts as long as possible plant the bulbs when still tight in bud.

pot et fleur

FLOWERS

1. 1 *Ficus pumila* plant
2. 1 *Helxine soleirolii* plant
3. 1 *Dracena marginata* plant
4. 1 stem Cymbidium Orchids

1   2

3   4

A *pot et fleur* is a collection of foliage plants with added cut flowers. A water-holding receptacle is hidden in the soil for the flowers. This type of design is ideal for an office, waiting room, or reception area, because even when the flowers have gone, the arrangement will still look good and continue to grow if it is cared for. Larger, bold flowers will have more impact in this type of design. Choose plants which will live happily together.

Difficulty: Intermediate

METHOD

1 Use chippings in the bottom of the container to provide drainage, then fill the container approximately half full with soil. Insert the test tube into the soil at the back of the container, so that the top of the tube is level with the rim of the container.

Use a soil which will suit the chosen plants. There are many universal mixtures available, if unsure ask the advice of your local florist.

2 Carefully tap the bottom of the pot holding the dracena to loosen the root ball. Remove the plant from its pot. Try to keep the soil around the root ball in one piece, then place at the back of the container. In the same way carefully remove the ficus from its pot and place at the front of the arrangement. The trails should creep over the side of the container.

OTHER MATERIALS

1 container, 10 inches high
7-inch test tube
Potting soil and chippings
Carpet moss (*Minum* sp.)

If you are using a container without drainage holes it is essential to add a good layer of drainage material to the container first, otherwise the soil will become waterlogged. Broken crockery, chippings or grit will be perfect.

A pot et fleur is a traditional design. Here it is given an up-date by using strong sculptural plants and a modern lime green container. The cymbidium orchids complement the plants and container perfectly.

3 Add the helxine at the side of the container. Fill in any gaps around the plants with more soil then press all the soil down firmly. Cover the soil with moss, and fill up the test tube with water. Water the soil lightly and leave to drain. Insert the stem of orchids into the test tube, cutting the stem end diagonally. Top up the test tube with water every day.

Decide where you will place the arrangement, then look at the environment and choose plants which will live happily in the conditions of your room. To start with, choose plants which are easy to care for and will tolerate most conditions.

Last but not least never overwater, err on the dry side, use a moisture meter if unsure how much water to give the plants.

eleven

T H E   F O R E S T   F L O O R

THERE IS SOMETHING SPECIAL ABOUT WALKING THROUGH WOODS ON A BRIGHT FALL DAY, TRUDGING THROUGH THE FALLEN LEAVES, WITH THE CRUNCHING SOUND OF CRISP TWIGS BREAKING UNDERFOOT. HOW OFTEN DO WE LOOK DOWN OR EVEN NOTICE THE BEAUTY OF THE FOREST FLOOR? SEEING THE BEAUTY EVERYWHERE IN NATURE IS THE ESSENCE OF A GOOD FLOWER ARRANGER, AND DEVELOPING A SEEING EYE IS THE MOST IMPORTANT ACCOMPLISHMENT OF ALL.

IN THIS CHAPTER WE LOOK AT MOSSES AND LICHENS WHICH PLAY SUCH AN ESSENTIAL ROLE IN FLOWER ARRANGING. GONE ARE THE DAYS WHEN MOSS WAS ONLY USED AS A MEANS OF SUPPORTING THE FLOWERS, AND ALWAYS COVERED UP. TODAY THE BEAUTY OF MOSS WITH ITS SUBTLE SHADES OF GREENS, GRAYS, AND BROWNS, AND ITS FURRY TEXTURE IS AN IMPORTANT DESIGN ELEMENT IN ITS OWN RIGHT.

pine-cone tree

FLOWERS

1. 85 Pine-cones
2. 24 stems Wheat

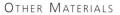

1   2

A pine-cone tree is an ideal decoration for fall and winter when flowers may be scarce or expensive. It can be decorated with wheat or fall leaves, and at Christmas burnished with gold spray paint, then decorated with evergreens. This arrangement has been placed on a terracotta pedestal to give it height.

Difficulty: Intermediate

METHOD

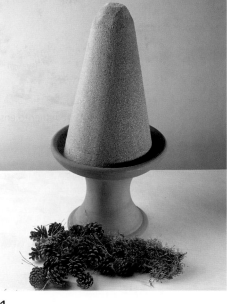

OTHER MATERIALS

Terracotta pedestal approx 12 inches high
Dry foam cone approx 24 inches high
2 bunches twigs
Raffia
7-inch stub wires
10-inch stub wires
Florist's adhesive fixing tape
Moss
Glue gun

1 Cut the point off the dry foam cone and cut into a dome shape. Press florist's adhesive tape down onto the terracotta pot and push the cone firmly onto it. Alternatively you can use a glue gun to fix the cone in place.

2 Wire the pine-cones by taking each cone and passing a seven-inch stub wire right around the scales at the base of the cone. Bring the two wires together and twist firmly and tightly at the base of the cone. The wire will have two legs which will give firm anchorage into the foam. Choose cones of a similar size to make the tree evenly shaped.

Gather pine-cones in the spring when they are fully open and falling from the trees naturally.

Use cedar cones for a flatter-shaped tree, or alternatively, use walnuts instead of cones, or a mixture of the two.

3 Cut the seven-inch wires in half and bend into hairpins. Choose flat pieces of moss and lay them on the cone starting at the base. Hairpin neatly through the moss and into the foam to hold the pieces in place. Cover all the foam cone with moss.

5 Continue adding pine-cones in lines neatly around the foam shape. Push the pine-cones tightly together to ensure the conical shape is maintained. Keep rotating the tree to ensure an even shape is achieved.

Entwine garlands of twigs around the cone to add a wilder look, or for a party, masses of trailing ivy for an opulent effect.

4 Start to add the cones. Place one of the best shaped pine-cones into the top of the dry foam to act as a guide. Then add the other pine-cones in lines, starting at the base. The first line should rest on the rim of the pedestal. Push both legs of wire firmly into the foam.

6 When all the pine-cones are in place, make four small wheatsheaves by taking bunches of six to eight stems of wheat and neatly graduating the heads to form a group. Tie with raffia, just below the heads. Trim the stalks to approximately twice the length of the heads.

A perfect thanksgiving decoration which can be adapted to reflect the changing seasons.

7 Cross two of the wheatsheaves in the center of a bundle of twigs. Take a ten-inch stub wire over the wheat and twigs to form a double-leg mount, securing all firmly together. Neatly cover this wire with raffia. Position the wheat and twigs at an angle, approximately one third from the top of the tree. Anchor into the tree by pushing the wires firmly through the pine cones and into the foam. Take the other bundle of twigs and wheatsheaves, tie together in the same way, with a long piece of raffia. Wrap the raffia around the base of the pedestal, tying firmly into place beneath the twigs.

Tie dried leaves to copper wires and thread between the pine-cones.

"And Winter, slumbering in the open air,
Wears on his smiling face a dream of Spring!"

SAMUEL TAYLOR COLERIDGE (1772 - 1834), *WORK WITHOUT HOPE*

hats off

FLOWERS

1. 6 Roses 'Leonardis' (*Rosa* sp.)
2. Ivy trails 'Glacier' and 'Little Eva' (*Hedra helix*)

1   2

OTHER MATERIALS

Straw hat, 15 inches diameter
Small piece of rope
Reel of binding wire
2 mini floral foam pads
Red reindeer moss (*Cladonia rangifera*)
Glue gun
10-inch stub wires

A lovely way to welcome friends to your home is to hang a decoration at the front door to show there is a warm reception waiting. This straw hat, made in a charming nostalgic fashion, is perfect for a garden party or *al fresco* meal. The cheery colors and leafy shade of the ivy create a bright and breezy effect guaranteed to bring out the sunshine.

Difficulty: Hard

METHOD

1 Using the glue gun, fix a small rope loop to the top underside of the hat. Hold the loop in place until the glue is dry. Make sure this loop is attached very securely. If necessary, a wire can be passed through the hat, close to the crown to give added anchorage to the loop.

2 Make a long band of reindeer moss by binding handfuls of moss together with wire in a firm, neat line (see steps 2–4 on pages 171–2). Make the band long enough to fit around the crown of the hat. Join the two ends of the band together when long enough to form a circle.

Moss is indispensable for the flower arranger. It makes a natural cover to hide mechanics, and will prove less fussy than foliage which can destroy the design if over-used.

3 Place the ring of moss around the crown of the hat. Make hairpins with stub wire, push these over the moss band and through the hat, twisting the ends together neatly on the back of the hat, and trimming off any excess wire. Four hairpins at equal distances around the hat should secure the moss band to the hat.

4 The mini foam pads have an adhesive strip on the plastic backing. Soak the foam then attach the two foam pads to the hat, one at the top and the other at the bottom slightly off center.

5 Take the trails of ivy, fix the stem ends into the foam and entwine the band of moss with ivy. Be generous with the ivy for a wild, country style.

Carpet moss and bunn moss can be allowed to dry out, and used in dried arrangements.

6 Make two more bands of moss approximately five inches in length, garland each band with a trail of ivy, then wire one of the ends of the moss band, making a double-leg mount.

If the moss looks very brown, a magical trick to bring it back to life is to place it in a bowl of boiling water. The moss reverts to its bright green color

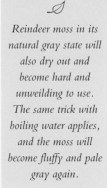

Reindeer moss in its natural gray state will also dry out and become hard and unweilding to use. The same trick with boiling water applies, and the moss will become fluffy and pale gray again.

A fine invitation to an open house, this old-fashioned garden hat will start the party off in a merry style.

7 Fix the two bands of moss to imitate streamers of ribbon. Push the wire mount through the hat, twist the wire together securely at the back and trim off any excess.

8 Add the roses in two groups into the foam to create areas of interest. Cut the stem ends diagonally and push well into the foam. Make sure all materials are secure, then hang from the rope loop.

the rose bower

FLOWERS

1. 20 Roses 'Hollywood' (*Rosa* sp.)
2. 3 long Ivy trails (*Hedera helix* 'Glacier')

1   2

OTHER MATERIALS

Bowl, 10 inches diameter, 6 inches deep
Piece of wire netting
Carpet moss (*Mnium* sp.)
Reel wire

This romantic arrangement of massed roses has a wreath of moss encircling the container, with ivy weaving through the design to lighten and separate the round forms of the roses. The greatest impact will be achieved by using roses of only one color. To help the roses last as long as possible, they are arranged in wire netting in a bowl of deep water.

Difficulty: Intermediate

METHOD

1 Crumple the wire netting up to form a web to support the flower stems. Push into the bowl, so that the inside is filled with netting. Fill the bowl with water.

2 Make a long band of moss. Take a handful of moss, tie the reel wire around the moss and secure by twisting the wire together. Add another handful of moss, tuck it into the first handful then bind into place with the reel wire, pulling the wire firmly toward you each time.

Hydrangea heads packed together then entwined with grass look stunning.

3 Keep adding moss in this way, binding closely and firmly together to produce a neat and tidy band of moss.

5 Trim off any untidy bits of moss, place the moss ring onto the rim of the container. It should sit securely in place.

Large white lily heads, entwined with ivy trails will also look fabulous.

4 Add moss until the band is long enough to sit around the top of the container. Keep measuring the moss band, it will fall off the container if it is too big. Bind the ends of the band together firmly to form a circle. Cut the wire and tuck the end into the moss.

6 Cut the rose stems diagonally and begin to place into the bowl with the stems anchored by the wire netting beneath. Start in the center of the bowl, and place five roses into the center in close formation.

8 Finally push the stem ends of ivy into the bowl of water, then thread the ivy trails through the arrangement with the tips trailing over the moss ring.

7 Keep adding roses, tucking them closely together. The roses around the edge of the arrangement should be placed slightly lower to give the arrangement a domed effect.

Using wire netting as mechanics for a flower arrangement is an ideal method for flowers which need a lot of water or dislike floral foam.

This is an ideal style of arrangement for old-fashioned garden roses. Their blowsy open heads perfectly suit this type of design. If using this arrangement on a dining table, scatter rose petals between the plates for pure romance and fragrance.

the swamp

Spheres of moss and ivy emerge from the damp steamy swamp in this arrangement, designed to create a study in form and texture. Pond weed floats around the spheres to enforce the feeling of lush vegetation, while tendrils of typha leaf form a vortex above the solid moss shapes. An unusual, restful sculptural arrangement which will work well on a low coffee-table.

Difficulty: Easy

FLOWERS

1. Typha leaves (*Liriope muscari*)
2. Ivy leaves (*Hedera helix* 'Glacie')

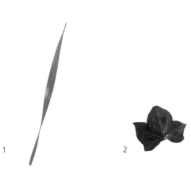

1   2

OTHER MATERIALS

Shallow glass bowl, 16 inches diameter
2 foam balls, 4 inches diameter
1 foam ball, 6 inches diameter
Pond weed
Carpet moss (*Mnium* sp.)
Reindeer moss (*Cladonia rangifera*)
Reel of binding wire
10-inch stub wires
1-inch knob pins

METHOD

1 Start with a four inch ball. Attach the reel wire to the ball by wrapping it around the ball and twisting the wire together. Clean the reindeer moss, place on the top of the ball, then bind in place firmly with the wire. Keep adding moss and binding in place until the entire ball is covered. Cut the binding wire and push the end through the moss and into the ball to secure.

2 Take the six inch ball. Clean dirt and twigs from the carpet moss. Make hairpins with the stub wire. Place the moss onto the ball then hairpin into place. Make sure the moss is flat and follows the contours of the ball. Keep adding pieces of moss until the ball is covered. Make sure all the moss is securely hairpinned into place.

3 The third ball is covered with ivy leaves which are pinned into place. Choose ivy leaves which are approximately the same size. Cut one third off the bottom of the leaf. Start at the top of the ball, pin five leaves together with one pin at the top tips of the leaves. Add the leaves in circles. Overlap each leaf and pin into position neatly. Work down the ball, finishing off the end in the same way as the top.

5 The typha leaves should swirl above the arrangement. Add one leaf at a time. Push the stem end into one of the covered balls, bend the leaf in the desired direction, then hairpin the tip into place neatly. Keep adding the leaves until the encircling effect has been achieved.

The leaves create a whirlpool of motion above the solid forms of the spheres with the weed and water simulating the swamp.

4 Fill the container with water and add the pond weed. Arrange the balls onto the container, with the water underneath.

"*...I must go seek some dewdrops here,
and hang a pearl in every cowslip's ear...*"

WILLIAM SHAKESPEARE (1564 - 1616), *A MIDSUMMER NIGHT'S DREAM*

left overs

FLOWERS

1. 2 Achillea (*Achillea* sp.)
2. 4 Allium 'Purple Sensation' (*Allium* sp.)
3. 2 Poppies (*Papaver* sp.)
4. 4 Mini Gerbera 'Purple Rain' (*Gerbera* sp.)
5. 2 Typha leaves (*Liriope muscari*)

1

2   3

4   5

Other Materials

2 ceramic water-tight pots, 5 inches high
12 kumquats
Reel of binding wire
Reel of pink wire
Carpet moss (*Mnium* sp.)

There are often one or two blooms left over from other arrangements that will be discarded. Similarly, garden flowers do not always grow in a profusion and there is frequently just one or two different varieties of flowers. This quirky little arrangement shows how to use these left-overs in a bright, fun way which will bring a smile to people's faces.

Difficulty: Easy

METHOD

1 Make two moss rings to fit snugly on the tops of the pots. Make these in the same way as the one made in the Rose Bower (see page 171).

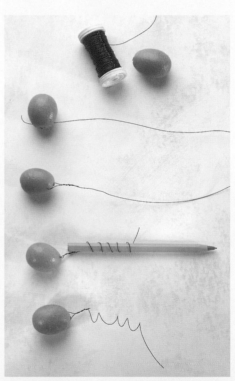

2 Wire the kumquats by taking a length of pink wire, threading it through the base of the fruit until an inch of wire protrudes on the other side. Twist this short end tightly onto the other wire at the base of the kumquat. To make a curled effect, wrap the wire loosely around a pen, then pull the pen through leaving a curly wire.

4 Fill the pots with water, then add the gerbera and the alliums around the edge of the container with the heads resting on the moss ring.

5 Add the poppies in the center and tuck the achillea in between the alliums and gerberas. Wind pink reel wire up two typha leaves for a decorative effect. Then link both pots together by placing the ends of the typha leaves in one pot, looping the leaves and pushing the tips into the other pot.

3 Attach six kumquats to each moss ring, evenly spacing them out around the pot. Take the wire over the moss ring and secure by pushing it into the moss. The kumquats will dance around the sides of the pots.

Joining simple pots together is an ideal way to make a long table center. Use enough pots to stretch the length of the table for an impressive effect, which is inexpensive to achieve and has a bright style.

twelve

JOYFUL OCCASIONS

SPECIAL EVENTS AND FEASTDAYS GIVE US CAUSE TO CELEBRATE. THROUGHOUT THE YEAR, HAPPY OCCASIONS ARE MARKED BY GATHERING TOGETHER FAMILY AND FRIENDS TO TOAST THESE SPECIAL DAYS. WHETHER IT'S A FORMAL ANNIVERSARY OR SPUR-OF-THE-MOMENT AL FRESCO EATING, FLOWERS WILL GIVE THE PARTY PANACHE. FLOWERS ARE GIVEN AND RECEIVED AT ALL THE MOST IMPORTANT TIMES OF OUR LIVES, THEY WILL SPEAK WHEN WORDS FAIL US, AND THE TRADITIONS ASSOCIATED WITH THEM SHOULD NEVER BE UNDERESTIMATED. THIS CHAPTER BRINGS TOGETHER THOSE MOST IMPORTANT OCCASIONS, WITH SEASONAL IDEAS TO DECORATE THE HOME.

christmas door wreath

FLOWERS

1. Cupressus (*Cupressus* sp.)
2. Variegated Holly (*Ilex* sp.)
3. Blue Pine (*Abies nobilis*)

1

2

3

OTHER MATERIALS

12-inch wire wreath frame
Roll of wreath wrap
Spaghnum moss
Green gutter percha
Raffia
Small bundles of twigs
Ribbon, plain red and tartan
Pine-cones
Orange slices
Reel wire
12-inch and 7-inch stub wires

A Christmas door wreath is the most traditional form of seasonal decoration. There are certain technical considerations to adhere to when making a door decoration. The finished wreath must have a secure hook attached to the frame for firm anchorage to the door. It can also take a battering from the weather once hung on the front door, so all foliage and embellishments must be waterproof and firmly attached to the base.

Difficulty: Intermediate

METHOD

1 Attach the reel wire securely to the wreath frame, and bind in handfuls of moss, pushing each section up snugly to the previous one. Continue until the frame is evenly mossed.

2 Attach the wreath wrap to the underside of the wreath, on the inner side, hairpinning in place. Bring the wreath wrap back over the moss at a slight angle and hairpin to the outer edge. Take the wreath wrap back over to the inner edge at an angle and hairpin again. Continue in this zigzag way until all the back of the frame is covered with a protective coat of plastic.

This moss ring can be used as the base for many door wreath designs.

3 Make a strong hook by guttering together two twelve-inch stub wires (see page 18). Pass the wire through the moss and under the outer wire ring. Twist the two wire ends together to form a loop. Wind the wire ends into the loop and cut off any excess wire. Then gutter over the whole loop to make it neat and secure.

5 Add the cupressus to the outer edge of the ring first. Push the two wires into the moss, with the cupressus facing away from you, then bend the wire so that the cupressus faces you and lies flat at the edge of the wreath, hooking into the moss securely.

4 Wire up approximately thirty-five to forty small bunches of cupressus for the edging and the center of the wreath. The cupressus should be approximately two and a half inches long. Wire in the double-leg method with a seven-inch length wire, by bending the wire in half at the middle, place the bent wire at the back of the cupressus, bring one wire round and wrap firmly around the base of the cupressus and the other wire (see page 20). When finished there should be two wire legs to push into the moss.

6 Continue around the outer edge angling the cupressus downward so that it touches the table top, and forms a neat circle of foliage all around the wreath.

7 Add more cupressus in the same way to the inner edge, taking care not to obscure the hole in the center of the wreath.

9 Once the wreath is full of evergreens and all the moss covered, wire the bundles of sticks, slices of orange, and pine-cones in the double-leg method and add in even groups around the top of the wreath, again bending and hooking the wires into the moss for safe anchorage.

8 Wire up bunches of holly and blue pine in the double-leg method. Use these and cupressus to cover the top of the moss, again hooking the wires into the moss securely. Use groups of the three evergreens to form patterns around the wreath, laying the foliage flat so that it does not stand up too tall.

The door wreath dates back to pagan times when boughs of evergreens would be hung on outer doors as protection against evil spirits.

10 Make a large bow of red velvet ribbon with streamers and add into the center of this a smaller bow of tartan ribbon (see page 22). Wire firmly together using the double-leg technique with a twelve-inch stub wire. Hold the wreath at the top by the hook, then position the bow at the center top of the wreath, push the two wires straight through the wreath to protrude from the back. Bend the wires and push them back into the moss base to form a neat stitch at the back, cutting off any excess wire. This will anchor the bow firmly to the wreath. Spray with water daily.

For another variation, use ivy and its berries with shiny green apples. Frost the tips of the leaves and apples with eggwhite and sugar.

For a different look, make the mixed evergreen base. Push cloves into tangerines then wire these firmly to the base. Finish with natural raffia bows for a rustic look.

Hanging a door decoration at Christmas is a time-honored way to greet passers-by and welcome guests. This door wreath not only looks festive, it also has the wonderful aroma of pine-cones and citrus fruits.

christmas glow

FLOWERS

1. 10 Roses 'Cappucino' (*Rosa* sp.)
2. 5 stems Hypericum 'Pinky Flair'
3. Variegated Holly (*Ilex* sp.)

1

2

3

This festive arrangement will bring a golden glow to the Christmas table. A gold platter laden with pine-cones, watched over by a wooden reindeer, with holly and golden roses nestling between the cones. Finished with shimmering gold candles, it combines glamor with the rustic appeal of traditional Christmas decorations.

Difficulty: Easy

METHOD

OTHER MATERIALS

Gold dish, 13 inches diameter
Floral foam
2 gold candle tapers, 13 inches long
2 gold candles, 10 inches long
1 wooden reindeer
2 small gold star candles
2 large star candles
Selection of pine-cones
Plastic foam holder with florist's fixing tape
Two-sided cream and gold stiffened ribbon

1 Fasten the foam holder onto the dish with florist's fixing adhesive. Push a piece of soaked floral foam onto the holder. Position the candles to one side of the foam, at varying heights, pushing them firmly into the foam. The reindeer stands to the back of the candles; push the legs of the reindeer into the foam firmly. Place two star candles on opposite sides of the container. A small piece of florist's fixing adhesive secures the candles in place if necessary.

Candles can be a fire hazard.
Make sure that all flowers, foliage, and artificial
materials are well away from the flame.
Never leave lighted candles unattended.
Extinguish before the candles burn too low.

The shimmer of golden candles will add the Midas touch to your Christmas table. Finish each napkin by tying with the same cream and gold ribbon, then add a gold rose to each one.

2 Pile up the pine-cones on top of the foam and around the edges of the container. Choose different shaped cones for added interest. Make a figure-of-eight bow with the ribbon, wire in the double-leg method (see page 22). Position the bow in front of the candles with the wire legs pushed into the foam.

3 Add the roses in groups, peeping out from the cones. Cut the stem ends diagonally and push the stems firmly into the foam. Then position the holly and hypericum around the edges of the container, between the cones. Finish by placing the small star candles into the arrangement around the edge of the container.

mother's day posy

FLOWERS

1. 20 stems Grape Hyacinths (*Muscari* sp.)
2. 5 *Bupluerum griffithii*
3. 20 stems Forget-me-nots (*Mysotis* sp.)
4. 3 *Viburnum opulus*
5. 3 Lizianthus (*Eustoma russellianum*)
6. 6 Roses 'Souvenir' (*Rosa* sp.)
7. 10 Narcissi 'Cheerfulness' (*Narcissi* sp.)
8. Bear grass (*Xerophyllum tenax*)

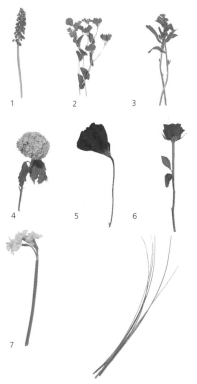

1   2   3

4   5   6

7

OTHER MATERIALS

Twine or raffia
Ribbon

In centuries past, young people would leave home to go away to work as apprentices or domestic servants. They were expected to work every day but it was the custom to allow them one Sunday off to go to visit their parents. They would pick flowers on the way home as gifts for their mother, and so this day became known as Mothering Sunday. The custom continues today and we all like to honor our own mothers in some way on this special day. The best present is a gift you have made yourself, and by producing your own posy with your mother's favorite flowers you are giving a unique offering of love.

Difficulty: Intermediate

METHOD

1 Clean the stems and remove any foliage that will fall below the tying point, then lay out the flowers in groups on the work bench for easy access when working.

3 Group the lizianthus and viburnum closely to the central roses to start the circular shape.

2 Take the roses and group with the heads together in a compact circle. Hold in the hand where the tying point will be.

4 To achieve neat spiralling stems feed the flowers in from left to right at the front and from right to left at the back. Continue to add the narcissi and grape hyacinths in compact groups all at the same level.

6 Take groups of bear grass and form loops around the edge of the bouquet to make a frill effect around the flowers.

7 Cut off a long length of twine or raffia, double it, and place around the stems. Draw the two ends of the twine through the loop and pull firmly. Divide the twine ends and wrap around the stems, pull tightly and tie with a double knot.

8 Finish the posy by cutting the stems neatly, the posy will stand on its stems if they are cut into an inverted 'V' shape. Attach a ribbon bow, in a color to enhance the flowers, around the tying point to give a neat effect (see page 23).

5 Making sure you keep the circular shape, add the final flowers, forget-me-nots and bupleurum, still spiralling the stems and gradually lowering the height of the flowers around the edge of the posy to give a domed shape and good profile.

The charm of old-fashioned flowers tied in a simple posy says "I love you" in a personal way which will delight any mother.

"*Sweet spring, full of sweet days and roses*"

GEORGE HERBERT (1593 - 1633), *VIRTUE*

easter

FLOWERS

1. 5 Gerbera 'Delphi' (*Gerbera* sp.)
2. 5 Roses 'Cream Prophyta' (*Rosa* sp.)
3. 10 Tulips (*Tulipa* sp.)
4. Mimosa (*Acacia dealbata*)
5. Eucalyptus (*Eucalyptus* sp.)
6. Leather leaf (*Arachniodes adianti formis*)
7. Bear grass (*Xerophyllum tenax*)
8. Galax leaves (*Galax viceolata*)

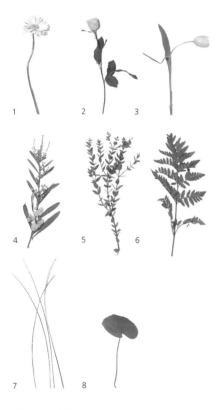

1   2   3

4   5   6

7   8

OTHER MATERIALS

Basket with a waterproof liner, 8 inches diameter,
   3½ inches deep
Floral foam
2 artificial nests with eggs
A few larger artificial eggs on wires
18-inch stub wires
Rubber band
Plastic floral foam holder with sticky fix-on

Easter is a joyous occasion; places of worship are decorated with traditional white lilies, and the fresh, young colors of yellow and white are associated with Eastertide. It is a time for giving and receiving gifts of flowers, and the custom of giving eggs at Easter is centuries old. It is therefore appropriate to decorate our homes with these items at this time of year, and this arrangement captures the essence of Easter. It will make an ideal table center for Easter Sunday lunch.

Difficulty: Intermediate

METHOD

1 Take one of the long stub wires, push it through the base of the artificial nest, then back through to form two legs. Twist the legs together at the top. Wire the other nest in the same way.

2 Put the foam holder in the middle of the basket then push the wet foam onto it. The foam should rise at least an inch above the rim of the basket. Anchor the foam in the basket with a rubber band, stretching it around the handles of the basket for security.

3 Add the eucalyptus to form an even outline around the basket, pushing the stems into the sides of the foam. Remove any leaves from the bottom of the stems for easy insertion into the foam. Add eucalyptus to the center to establish the height, which for a posy-type arrangement should be approximately the same length as the side pieces.

4 Add the leather leaf next to cover the foam, with the galax leaves placed around the edge, with one or two in the center.

5 Push the egg nests into either side of the foam, positioning them so that they tip over the edge of the basket. Next, add one rose to the center of the arrangement with the others grouped around it. The roses will be the tallest flowers in the arrangement.

6 The tulips are inserted into the foam next, with some falling over the edge of the basket and one or two into the center of the arrangement.

7 The gerbera are inset slightly into the arrangement to give depth. Fill in with mimosa to strengthen the outline, and give textural interest.

8 Add wisps of bear grass to give movement to the design and tuck the eggs into the center of the arrangement.

Place the arrangement in the center of the dining table for a perfect Easter look.

lasting love

The most romantic day of the year is St Valentine's Day, when couples profess their love for each other with gifts of flowers and cards. The red rose has become the symbol of true love, and therefore the most appropriate flower to give. In this long-lasting planted arrangement, the miniature red roses are surrounded by a heart of ivy, then finished with gingham ribbon.

Difficulty: Intermediate

FLOWERS

1. 2 Ivy 'Kolibri' plants (*Hedera helix*)
2. 3 miniature red Rose plants (*Rosa* sp.)

OTHER MATERIALS

Red wooden container, approx 9 inches square
Metal heart frame, 15 inches high
Plastic sheeting
Soil and gravel
Red gingham ribbon, 2½ inches wide
Red raffia
Carpet moss (*Mnium* sp.)
Glue gun

METHOD

1 Using a glue gun, attach the wide gingham ribbon to the sides of the container with a small amount of glue. Line the wooden container with strong plastic sheeting. Add a layer of gravel or broken clay pots into the base for drainage, then a thin layer of soil over the top.

2 Tap out the rose bushes from their pots and plant in the center of the container.

3 Add the heart frame to the container, pushing the point well into the soil in the center, between the rose bushes. Then plant one ivy at the side of the arrangement.

5 Plant another ivy at the other side of the heart and wind the trails around the frame as before, so that the entire heart frame is covered with ivy. Add more soil around the plants and firm the soil in well.

4 Wind the trails of ivy around the heart frame to the center point. Tie in place with raffia if necessary to secure.

The planted roses must be watered regularly to ensure they last as long as possible.

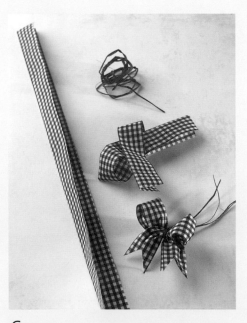

6 Make a bow by taking fifteen inches of ribbon. Fold the wide ribbon in half lengthways, then make a figure-of-eight with it. Take a small piece of red raffia, pinch the bow together in the center, wrap the raffia round this central point and tie firmly, leaving two ends of raffia (see page 23 for more details).

Guaranteed to set the heart a-flutter, this long-lasting Valentine is the perfect love token to send to the love in your life.

7 Use carpet moss to fill in around the edges of the container and give a neat finish. Water the soil lightly then add the gingham bow to the central point of the heart, tying in place firmly with the raffia ends.

for the bride

FLOWERS

1. 12 white Roses 'Grazz' (*Rosa* sp.)
2. 10 stems Cow Parsley 'Ami Majus' (*Amthriscus sylvestris*)
3. 5 stems white Spray Roses 'Princess' (*Rosa* sp.)
4. 15 stems *Alchemilla mollis*
5. Bear grass (*Xerophyllum tenax*)
6. Trails of Ivy (*Hedera helix*)

OTHER MATERIALS

Florist's twine or raffia
White organza ribbon, 2 inches wide
Cream decorative ribbon, ½ inch wide
Glue gun

Bridal bouquets require much more technical skill to make than other forms of floral art and unless you are very competent, anything other than a small hand-tied posy should be left to a professional florist who will have spent many years perfecting the art of bridal floristry. This hand-tied bouquet in the bridal colors of creams and whites is ideal for a small summer wedding where the bride wishes to carry a loose, natural bouquet.

Difficulty: Hard

METHOD

2 Start adding the roses and spray roses, using cow parsley and alchemilla in between to produce a rounded open effect. Add bear grass and loop back into the tying point, around the focal flowers.

1 Lay all the materials on a table and clean the stems, removing any foliage which will be below the tying point. Take a small bunch of alchemilla and cow parsley. Bridal bouquets should not be too tall, no more than nine inches from the tying point to the top flower.

3 Make sure the stems spiral neatly by adding flowers and foliage at the front of the bouquet from left to right, and at the back from right to left. In this way all stems angle the same way. Keep adding the roses and filler materials, reducing the length of stem so that the flowers come down to the hand, giving a rounded profile.

6 Cut the stems to approximately one third the size of the bouquet, in an inverted "V" shape. Make a figure-of-eight bow with the widest ribbon, then, holding this in the hand make another figure-of-eight bow with the narrower ribbon on top of the first bow. Take a long length of narrow ribbon and tie the bows together using the method shown on page 23. Place the bow over the tying point, take the two long ribbon ties around and tie securely above the bow at the front. Add the ribbon and rose trails by pushing the double-leg wire firmly into the front of the bouquet until no wire shows.

The effect is a very natural country style, perfect for the bride who wants a "just picked" look.

4 Add the ivy trails evenly around the edges with groups of bear grass in between. Tie securely with twine or raffia (see page 24).

5 Cut three long trails of the narrow ribbon to different lengths. Wire the three ribbons together with a double-leg mount. Use the glue gun to attach a small spray rose to each ribbon.

baby blues

New arrivals bring great joy, and this happy occasion should be marked in some special way. What better than a personally made arrangement of flowers? In this mother and baby arrangement, mossy teddybears make the focal areas and the arrangements are linked by a symbolic "cord" of limonium. This will surely delight the proud parents.

Difficulty: Intermediate

FLOWERS

1. 4 stems Lizianthus (*Eustoma russellianum*)
2. 5 stems Freesia 'Blue Heaven' (*Freesia* sp.)
3. 10 stems *Limonium latifollium* 'Emille'
4. 5 stems Columbine (*Aquilegia* sp.)
5. Ivy (*Hedera helix*)

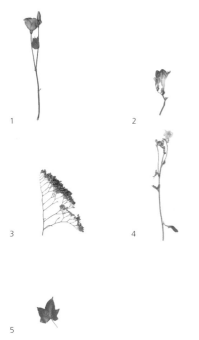

1

2

3

4

5

OTHER MATERIALS

2 containers, 8 inches high, 6 inches high
Floral foam
Reel of binding wire
2 moss teddybears on sticks
Ribbon
Raffia

METHOD

1 Cut the limonium into pieces approximately four inches long. Make a small bunch and attach the binding wire firmly to the stem just below the flower heads.

2 Keep binding down the stems adding small bunches of limonium until the garland is long enough to form an arch between the two arrangements, approximately thirty-six inches long. Keep pulling the wire tightly to make a firm binding around the limonium.

3 Fill the containers with foam. The foam should stand one inch above the top of the containers. Position the containers and fix the limonium archway to both containers by tying with raffia.

In the warm environment of a hospital, flowers will drink more water so will need topping up with water daily.

5 Tie bows around the teddybears' necks. Push the sticks with the teddybears into the center of the foam. The teddybears should sit right down, on the foam.

4 Fill in around the base of the arrangement with ivy leaves, pushing the stems firmly into the foam. Add any remaining limonium to the sides and back of the foam.

6 Take the columbine and freesia and place them around the teddybears in groups, to form an outline.

7 Group the lizianthus beneath the teddybears, to draw the eye to the focal areas. With the ribbon make two bows with streamers (see page 22). Add these below the teddybears to trail down the front of the containers.

If space is at a premium in the hospital, the arrangement can be reduced to a single container with an arch over the bear.

Welcome the new arrival with a beautiful gift for both mother and baby which will thrill and delight the new parents.

midsummer's dream

FLOWERS

1. 3 *Allium aflatunense* 'Purple Sensation'
2. 4 Delphinium 'Belladonna' (*Delphinium* sp.)
3. 7 Sweet Peas (*Lathyrus odoratus*)
4. 10 *Scabious caucasica*
5. 10 Pinks (*Dianthus* sp.)
6. 1 stem pale pink Lily 'La Reve' (*Lilium* sp.)
7. 2 stems *Alchemilla mollis*
8. 2 stems Hebe (*Hebe* sp.)
9. Ivy trails (*Hedera helix*)
10. Ivy trails (*Hedera erectica*)
11. *Senecio greyii*
12. 5 Pennisetum (*Pennisetum* sp.)

OTHER MATERIALS

Terracotta trough	Floral foam
5 x 12 inches	Plastic sheeting

Celebrate summer with this lovely indoor herbaceous border. The tall flower spikes of delphinium, with the round heads of the allium form the backdrop of the border. Grouped in front, the fragrant lilies, sweet peas, and pinks, form a soft profusion of summer colors.

Difficulty: Easy

METHOD

1 Line the terracotta trough with strong plastic sheeting to provide a watertight liner. Use enough wet floral foam to fill the trough, the foam should stand at least two inches above the rim of the container.

2 Using the tallest flowers first, make two parallel groups at either end of the foam. Graduate the length of stem slightly, and cut the stem ends diagonally.

4 Add the sweet peas in a shorter group at the front of the foam between the delphiniums and alliums. Cut the open flowers from the lily stem and use at the front of the foam, to one side with the buds placed at the back of the open flowers.

3 Make a group of hebe next to the alliums at the back of the foam, with a group of senecio at the opposite end of the arrangement. Fill in the front of the arrangement with trails of ivy, to cascade over the rim of the trough.

This style of arrangement can be used to imitate many natural landscapes. Try making a cornfield scattered with bright red poppies.

5 The pinks and scabious are used in natural groups as though they were growing in a border.

6 The lime-green alchemilla will blend with the summer colors perfectly, with the wispy grass pennisetum grouped into the center and side of the arrangement. Make sure all the foam is covered and the back of the arrangement is finished off neatly.

The heady scent of summer in an enchanting collection of herbaceous plants makes a summer garden come alive indoors.

"*All dear Nature's children sweet
Lie 'fore bride and bridegroom's feet,
Not an angel of the air,
Bird melodious or bird fair,
Be absent hence.*"

WILLIAM SHAKESPEARE *(1564 - 1616), A BRIDAL SONG*

Index

ACKNOWLEDGMENTS

Special people enrich our lives with their love, support and help. I am fortunate to have a family whose love and care know no bounds. My adoring love and thanks must go to my husband Ray, my son Tim and my wonderful parents, Joan and Gil Saunders, without whom nothing is possible. For her total support and help, my special thanks go to my best friend Linda Sharp. Thank you also to Pat Barkley for being such an inspirational friend. My appreciation and thanks to the staff of Floral Roundabout for smoothing the way for me.

My gratitude to the following companies for supplying the containers and sundries for this book.

CONTAINERS

Floral Roundabout,
59, Sidbury,
Worcester WR1 2HU

Fleur,
3 Station Parade,
Virginia Water,
Surrey, GU25 4AA

G. R. Pratley and Sons,
The Shambles,
Worcester

Barkley Arts,
Stourbridge,
Worcestershire

Floral Foam
Trident Foam Ltd.,
Marple Road,
Offerton,
Stockport, Cheshire, SK2 5HW

Dutch Auction and Shops Photography
Flower Council of Holland,
Catherine Chambers,
6–8 Catherine Street,
Salisbury,
Wiltshire SP1 2DA